Insect-Eating Lizards

Complete Herp Care

Philip Purser

Insect-Eating Lizards

For my wife, Jenny, whose faith has been "a light in dark places when all other lights go out." Thanks.

Project Team
Editor: Thomas Mazorlig
Copy Editor: Neal Pronek
Indexer: Lucie Haskins
Cover Design: Mary Ann Kahn
Design: Patti Escabi

T.F.H. Publications
President/CEO: Glen S. Axelrod
Executive Vice President: Mark E. Johnson
Publisher: Christopher T. Reggio
Production Manager: Kathy Bontz

T.F.H. Publications, Inc.
One TFH Plaza
Third and Union Avenues
Neptune City, NJ 07753

Copyright © 2008 by T.F.H. Publications, Inc.

All rights reserved. No part of this publication may be reproduced, stored, or transmitted in any form, or by any means electronic, mechanical or otherwise, without written permission from T.F.H. Publications, except where permitted by law. Requests for permission or further information should be directed to the above address.

Printed and bound in China,
08 09 10 11 12   1 3 5 7 9 8 6 4 2

ISBN 978-0-7938-2896-8

Library of Congress Cataloging-in-Publication Data
Purser, Philip.
  Insect-eating lizards : a complete guide to insectivorous lizards / Philip Purser.
      p. cm. -- (Complete herp care)
  Includes index.
  ISBN 978-0-7938-2896-8 (alk. paper)
  1. Lizards as pets. I. Title.
SF459.L5P875 2008
639.3'95--dc22

                              2007048126

This book has been published with the intent to provide accurate and authoritative information in regard to the subject matter within. While every reasonable precaution has been taken in preparation of this book, the author and publisher expressly disclaim responsibility for any errors, omissions, or adverse effects arising from the use or application of the information contained herein. The techniques and suggestions are used at the reader's discretion and are not to be considered a substitute for veterinary care. If you suspect a medical problem consult your veterinarian.

The Leader In Responsible Animal Care For Over 50 Years!®
www.tfh.com

Table of Contents

The explosion-shaped ad declared "Raise Chameleons for Fun & Profit," in bold-face print in the back of my Batman comic book. Beside the bold print was a caricature of a boy with a wad of cash in his hand and a small green lizard perched happily atop his shoulder. Both the boy and the lizard were smiling. I carefully cut the ad from the back of my comic book, slid it into an envelope along with $1.55, and ran outside to stick it in the mailbox.

Roughly eight weeks later, a small brown box arrived. It had two dozen tiny holes cut in the sides and bore a stamp reading "CAUTION: LIVE CHAMELEON" on its top. My stomach knotted in anticipation as I carefully opened the box, removed a vertical cardboard insert, and found resting in the bottom of the box a small brown lizard. I immediately took my "chameleon" upstairs and put it into my terrarium, and I began scheming as to how this little fellow would earn me that "profit" the comic book ad had boasted of.

Three days later my "chameleon" was dead.

I was eight years old, and the "chameleon" that the comic book advertisers had sent me was not a true chameleon but a green anole instead. I didn't learn that until a decade later. The green anole, in fact, was nowhere near a true chameleon; the two species have next to no shared characteristics, and they are only distantly related. The only similarity between the two species, and the reason the advertisers could get away with their false ad, is that both anoles and chameleons are capable of varying degrees of color change.

Introduction

But there is one more common factor between the true chameleon, which I thought I had received, and the green anole that lay motionless in the bottom of the box that I had actually received. They are both insectivorous lizards. The word insectivorous means "insect-eating," and it applies to a tremendous variety of lizards from around the world. From geckos to skinks to agamids and beyond, literally thousands of small to moderately sized lizards share the common characteristic of dining during just about every meal on six-legged (sometimes more-legged) prey. The simple fact of a shared diet translates to a skill set of husbandry knowledge that covers a wide range of potential pet lizards: once you learn how to properly care for one type of insectivorous lizard, you are largely equipped with the skills and know-how to care for many other species. And the best part about it is that insectivorous lizards, because of their wide variety and physical diversity, present a wide range of fun and exciting challenges to hobbyists of all skill levels; from the novice herp keeper who houses a pair of green anoles to the veteran who maintains a breeding colony of curly-tailed lizards, there is truly something for everyone in the world of insectivorous lizards!

And that's just where this book comes in. I wrote it as a handy resource guide for anyone—reptile expert or beginner—who is interested in learning more about the wide array of insect-eating lizards available in the pet trade today. So don't be afraid to bend back the cover, dog-ear the pages, and generally wear this book out. I wrote it to be used and referred to often. May it answer the questions, solve the problems, and eliminate the dilemmas that arise in all your endeavors in keeping insectivorous lizards.

Chapter 1

Acquiring Your Lizard

The first step in establishing a thriving colony of insect-eating lizards, or in selecting just the right specimen for a single-pet endeavor, is the acquisition step. Where and how you acquire your reptilian friend will partially determine the longevity, fruitfulness, and ultimate success of your relationship with your lizards. And since we all want to have as much quality time with our herps as possible, it's easy to see why the acquisition phase is so important.

Narrowing the Choices

Before you decide on how to acquire your pet lizard, you should first decide on what species you want, or at least what environment that species will come from. For example, do you want to keep desert-dwelling lizards? These animals typically require more heat and higher wattage ultraviolet UV light bulbs than do some species hailing from other habitats. This additional heat/light requirement may translate into a higher utility bill and initial expense in establishing the lizard's environment. Or do you prefer to keep a nocturnal species of lizard, such as a tokay gecko, which requires heat but very little UV lighting. Desert species will be much more visible during the day, but the nocturnal species will cost considerably less money to maintain.

Understand the needs of your lizard before you purchase it. A hardy forest-dweller, such as this panther gecko (*Paroedura pictus,* above), needs a much different terrarium than the delicate desert-dwelling Texas horned lizard (*Phrynosoma cornutum,* below).

Size is also a major consideration. You may well adore the arboreal geckos of Asia, but do you have adequate space to support as large a terrarium as these lizards require? Or are you looking for a desktop buddy? A small grassland or savanna-dwelling skink could make a perfect small-space specimen for the enthusiast who has limitations on space.In the end, everything is a matter of give-and-take, and by answering a few basic questions about how much time, space, and money you can realistically give to your new lizards, you can determine with great accuracy which species are right for you.

The back half of this book is dedicated to answering just those questions. Before you read much further, I recommend flipping to the section on species profiles and reading about the lizards that pique your interest. Of course, there are many more species available than what I have listed, and you can find more information about various species on the Internet (there are many reptile-related websites) or by talking to the folks that work with lizards at your local pet store.

Sources of Lizards

There are three avenues that you might take in acquiring your pet lizard: the local pet shop, the online retailer, and the herp expo. Each of these venues has its pros and its cons, and one or another of these sources may be highly more advantageous to your needs.

Pet Stores

The first avenue is the local pet shop. These stores range from the traditional "mom and pop" operation to the chain superstores. Local pet shops are, in most instances, the best way for beginning hobbyists to acquire their livestock, for not only can you physically inspect the animal or animals you might be interested in purchasing, but also most local pet stores have some variety of return policy. The return policy on livestock will vary from store to store, so be sure you understand exactly what that policy is before you make a purchase at a given store.

Once you enter the pet shop, survey all the reptile tanks and terrariums for general signs of good health among the livestock there. Do all the reptiles and amphibians seem healthy? Do they behave normally? Do any of the herps look too thin? Are their eyes closed or sunken? Are the terrariums clean and vibrantly lit, or are they cold, dark, or filthy with feces? How crowded are the tanks? As a general rule of thumb, lizards that are housed singly or in small numbers are in better health than lizards housed en masse in communal terrariums. Crowded animals are typically highly stressed, which will function to suppress their appetites and heighten risk of disease. I personally avoid purchasing lizards from crowded terrariums, and I recommend that my readers do as well; it is simply smarter and less risky to do so.

Online Sources

The next avenue for potential purchase is the online retailer. In an age where so much of our lives revolve around the Internet, online reptile and amphibian vendors have come online in force. A major plus to online ordering is that you typically will have access to a much wider variety of species than you'll find in a local pet shop. Online retailers are highly specialized distributors or breeders who can often supply rare species for you. More experienced hobbyists who have a good knowledge of the lizards they want are usually the ones who order from online retailers.

One problem with online retailers is that any money that you may save in the price of the lizard itself is offset by the cost of shipping. Only in very specialized instances, such as when an experienced hobbyist orders a rare reptile or a very large number of reptiles for a flat shipping fee, does the online avenue really pay off.

Aside from the prohibitive cost of shipping, the online retailer also offers the buyer no chance to inspect the livestock before purchasing. Unless you order from a dealer who has his livestock individually photographed and cataloged online (which is becoming more common), you'll have no way of knowing what your lizard will look like, what its disposition is, or how it will behave in captivity.

Even more risky is the condition of the animal. Ordering online forces the buyer to trust completely the ethics of the seller. There are some steps, however, that you can take to ensure that your ordering experience is as successful as it can possibly be. First of all, find a reputable online dealer who has (and adheres to) a reasonable return policy and live-on-delivery guarantee. Try to find out how long this dealer has been in the business. Search for classified ads in the back of reptile and amphibian magazines, as most breeders who pay the money to advertise in a magazine are serious about their profession and very likely offer superior livestock. You might also want to do some digging around and see whether there are any reviews of your chosen seller. See what others in the hobby have to say about the dealer before making a purchase.

Should you choose to purchase online, you should beware of the reptile forum or swap-site. While you

A clean pet store with a knowledgeable staff is a good source for common lizards, such as curly-tails (*Leiocephalus schreibersi*).

Looking for Bugs

Here is one of my own herp-inspection secrets. This trick is vital to the acquisition of a healthy lizard, and it is very simple to perform. Start by getting a white paper towel. Don't use a patterned towel or a dyed one, as it will not give you the same results. Dampen the paper towel in lukewarm chemical-free water (no soaps, chlorine, etc.) and wrap the towel more or less (depending on how large the lizard is) around the lizard's body. Now gently stroke the paper towel backward from the head toward the tail. Repeat this maneuver several times. Now unwrap the paper towel and inspect it for external parasites.

What you are looking for are mites or ticks, which most often come in on wild-caught specimens. Ticks are easy to spot, as they are small, bulbous beasts that can easily be seen with the naked eye. Mites are much smaller than ticks, and they infest reptiles in far greater numbers. If mites are present, they will appear as tiny reddish, black, or gray flecks crawling on the paper towel. Of course, virtually any type of substrate debris that was stuck to the lizard's scales might appear to be a mite to the untrained eye. Watch any specks you see for a minute; if they begin to crawl around, they're mites.

Mites are insidious parasites that can suck a small lizard dry of its blood, and if one lizard in a terrarium has them, it is guaranteed that all lizards in the tank have them. Most hobbyists have also found that if one terrarium in a pet shop has mites, then almost all of the time at least some, if not all, of the other terrariums and their inhabitants are also infested with mites. Never purchase a lizard that has mites, and it is my recommendation that you not purchase any reptile from a store in which reptilian mites are present.

can find a unique variety of insectivorous lizards on such sites, bear in mind that you are dealing with individuals who may or may not be ethically sound in their advertising and selling practices. A great many people every year report negative outcomes when purchasing from a reptile forum. Again, try to find a seller that other hobbyists recommend.

Reptile Expos

A final avenue toward acquiring your pet lizard is my favorite of them all: the reptile expo (also called herp shows, reptile shows, and similar names). Reptile expos bring in professional breeders and collectors from all around the nation and around the globe to offer their reptiles at highly competitive prices. Usually held in conventions centers, auditoriums, and other large public gathering places, these

A herp expo is the best place to see some of the rarer lizard — such as this sungazer (*Cordylus giganteus*)—in person.

events boast row upon row of tables, booths, and stands that are absolutely loaded with reptiles and amphibians of all shapes and sizes. Not only is the variety of lizards for sale extensive, but you also get the added advantage of being able to physically inspect the specific lizards you are interested in before making purchase.

Buying from a specialized breeder at a herp expo has numerous benefits as well. Most breeders who vend at expos take their breeding and their animals very seriously. They have given their animals the best, and they pass the best livestock on to the buyer. Breeders are also excellent sources of detailed information about the animals they breed. Buying directly from a breeder is a little more expensive than buying from, say, a large-scale importer, but the extra expense is definitely worth it. Professional breeders often offer guarantees and services that importers do not. I recommend that any hobbyist looking for both a superior pet lizard and excellent advice purchase from a professional breeder at a reptile expo.

One of the only drawbacks to purchasing your lizards at a reptile expo is that all sales are final. Once the vendors have your cash in their hands, it's pretty well a done deal. And this is understandable, because reptile expos last for only a weekend or so. It is simply not practical for the vendors to offer a warranty on their livestock. Don't let this no return policy steer you away from purchasing at a reptile expo; some of the most positive experiences I've ever had in buying insectivorous lizards have occurred at reptile swap-meets. I've bought tanks, hide boxes (often referred to in the hobby as just plain "hides"), plants, and other décor for my terrariums at super-low prices, I've found exotic lizards that I could not find anywhere else, and I've even met and made friends with professional herpetologists, breeders, and other authors who specialize in reptile and amphibian books. You simply never know what you're going to run into next at a reptile expo. I recommend them to anyone, veteran and beginner alike.

Captive-Bred vs. Wild-Caught

It is important to ask about the lizard's origins. Was it bred in captivity or was it collected from the wild? Captive-bred specimens are, in most hobbyists' opinions, far more desirable, as

Transporting Your Lizards

Transporting your lizards from the pet shop or reptile expo to your home terrarium can be a very taxing and nerve-wracking experience for your new reptilian friend, but it doesn't have to be. By following these steps, you can help to make the transition from pet shop to home as smooth and as painless as possible.

- Transport your lizard in a closed opaque container; a cardboard box can be a good choice. Transporting in a clear container can cause stress to the lizard. If the lizard is in a dark container and cannot see the world moving around it, it will not stress out nearly as much.
- Place something inside the container with the lizard during transport, such as a small clean towel. This will prevent the lizard from sliding around inside the box or clawing vainly for a foothold on the container's floor. A lizard that feels attached to something and stable in its environment is more at ease than if it has nothing to cling to.
- Avoid loud sounds during transport. Being packed into a box and shuffled around is stressful enough without the added problem of sound.
- Avoid the desire to play with or handle your new friend during transport. Even if someone else is driving and you have both hands free, handling your lizard during transit is never a good idea, as the lizard will be stressed to some extent.

Captive-bred lizards are almost always healthier than their wild-caught counterparts, especially when dealing with a delicate species, such as a giant frog-eyed gecko (*Teratoscinsus keyserlingii*).

they have been receiving superior care from dedicated breeders since they hatched. Wild-caught specimens, conversely, have been collected from their native environments by reptile hunters, sold to a pet distributor, and then shipped on to the pet shop. These animals have been under tremendous stress, so their immune systems are likely depressed and their health may be going down. Similarly, it is virtually impossible for you to determine what sort of internal parasites the lizard may be infected with. Wild lizards, depending on their species and what part of the world they come from, may play host to a wide variety of internal parasites, and the signs of these parasites may become apparent only after you purchase the animal.

More and more lizard keepers are refusing to purchase wild-caught animals on moral and ecological grounds. Every specimen that is removed from its native environment is essentially lost to that environment: It will not reproduce there, it will not give rise to the next generation of its kind, and it will not be a potential food source for other animals in its native ecosystem. This can lead to local extinctions and legislated protection for a species.

For example, during the 1970s and 1980s, Mexican red-knee tarantulas *(Brachypelma smithi)* were imported into the United States by the tens of thousands each year. They filled pet shops from coast to coast, and they were a favorite stock creature in Hollywood horror films. Collectors traveled south of the border to find these spiders in huge numbers throughout the Mexican countryside. Now these beautiful spiders command a high price among tarantula enthusiasts, and the same geographic areas that once supported thousands of red-knees are now bereft of them. And these spiders aren't alone; a number of reptile and amphibian species have vanished from their native habitats due to unregulated collection for the booming pet industry. It is an all-around better idea to purchase captive-bred animals whenever possible. You get a healthier animal, the professional breeder stays in business, and wild populations of your chosen species are left to thrive in nature.

Closer Inspection

After you determine the lizard's origins, ask to take the lizard out to handle and inspect it. In the case of some species, however, this is not a practical suggestion. Tiny or very delicate species, very nervous species, or exceedingly aggressive species may not be easily or realistically handled. The vendor will usually know which species can be inspected in-hand, and which ones cannot. Additionally, you should have researched the species you want and have a good idea about whether handling is appropriate.

Once the lizard is out and in your hands, hold it gently but firmly. Make sure not to squeeze its midsection, as even the grip of a child can crush the organs of a small lizard. Take care not to put too much pressure on its tail, as most lizards will drop their tails quickly if they are grabbed or squeezed. Grasp the animal in such as manner that it feels

Not Just Insects

Although this book is about insectivorous lizards, that term is somewhat misleading. Most of these lizards actually will eat a wide range of invertebrates (including insects, spiders, millipedes, and more), and larger species will prey on small vertebrates as well. Most species will prey on anything small enough for them to catch and eat. For brevity, this book will use the word "insect" when referring to the diet of these lizards, and the reader should understand that the term means "insects and other invertebrates small enough for the lizard to eat."

secure in your hand; a small lizard is much less likely to wriggle or try to flee if all its feet are firmly anchored. A lizard that feels largely like it is in control is much more likely to sit quietly in your hand than one that feels threatened in your grasp.

While it sits in your hand, you can learn a number of things about the lizard. You can inspect it for health problems and get a good feel for jut how handle-friendly this individual is. It's easy to see how there are behavioral variations between lizard species, but after you've handled a few different individuals of the same species, you'll also come to understand that there can be tremendous behavioral variation between members of the same species. If you're looking for a very handle-friendly pet that you, or perhaps your children, can enjoy and handle, you'll definitely want to shy away from very wriggly or aggressive specimens. No matter how visually attractive such an animal is, it will not live up to your expectations in captivity and, ultimately, both it and you will be unhappy sharing a home.

Begin inspecting for physical health by watching the lizard move about in your hands. Does it hold its head up and its eyes open? Does it seem alert and aware of what is going on? Insectivorous lizards are very keen, alert lizards that are virtually always well aware of their surroundings. In the wild they must be on the lookout for small,

You may not be able to handle some aggressive lizards, such as tokay geckos (*Gekko gecko*), for a health inspection.

fast-moving prey items, and they must also be ever vigilant against predators, so a high level of alertness is one of their key strategies.

No matter the species, the lizard should do something in your hands: struggle, bite, or just cling tightly to your fingers. An insectivorous lizard that doesn't cling to you, one whose legs dangle limply, is definitely a sick, sick animal, and you'll want to avoid that specimen at all costs. Inspect the animal for crust or pus around the edges of its eyes, nose, and mouth; bear in mind, however, that many iguanid species rid their bodies of excess salt by snorting it out their noses, so a crystalline white "crust" around the nostrils of an iguanid species is not necessarily a warning sign that anything is wrong. Inspect the limbs for rigidity and solid musculature and inspect the belly and dorsum for burns, cuts, lesions, sores, or any other malady. Inspect also the lizard's cloaca (the opening at the base of the tail through which it excretes waste and through which reproductive activity, including the laying of eggs, takes place); the cloaca should be closed and clean around its edges. Very nervous specimens may actually excrete on you when you handle them; in such cases the cloaca is likely to still be slightly open when you get around to inspecting it!

Before you buy it, check a lizard's head for eye injuries, crust around the mouth, and other signs of illness. This Schneider's skink (*Eumeces schneideri*) looks healthy.

After you've found a strong, mild-mannered, and generally healthy-looking lizard, you may think it's time to go ahead and purchase this little fellow, right? Well, not exactly. A final step (although it is not a critical one) in inspecting any potential pet lizards is to watch it feed. This is generally only possible when buying a lizard from a pet store.

After you've handled it, put the lizard back into its terrarium and ask the shopkeeper when feeding time is, then come back at that time to see your chosen lizard eat. Bear in mind that even the most robust of lizards, unless it is very accustomed to human touch, will not likely feed immediately after being handled. Give the lizard at least a half hour or so to calm down before expecting it to eat. Most specimens will not hesitate to feed right in front of you, however, as insectivorous lizards are opportunistic feeders, Mother Nature has programmed them to feed almost every time they see a prey item nearby. Very full specimens (that fed earlier that day) may be hesitant to feed in your presence, and nocturnal species present a real challenge in this department. Nocturnal species, such as the very commonly kept house gecko, may not feed until deep into the dark hours of the night. Expecting to see one eat in captivity may not be a practical expectation.

As I said, seeing a potential pet lizard feed before making purchase is definitely a plus in ensuring that you are getting the healthiest animal possible (after all, what good is a lizard that refuses to feed? It won't last long in captivity if it doesn't.), but it is not crucial. Under normal circumstances, any insectivorous lizard that passes all the other health inspections will definitely feed regularly and heartily in the home terrarium.

Chapter 2

Housing, Heating, and Lighting

t is important to note that whatever species of lizard you choose and whatever type of habitat that species needs, it is absolutely imperative that you have that habitat ready *before* you bring your new lizard home. It is a cardinal sin to purchase any reptile without having first established the home terrarium in which your cold-blooded companion will live. Transport from the pet shop to your home is stressful enough for your small lizards, so a quick, smooth transition into a warm, well equipped, and hospitable home is a must to ensure the proper acclimation of your new pet to its new home. But just exactly what type of terrarium you construct will depend on a great many factors.

Caging Options

Most hobbyists house their lizards in all-glass aquariums or glass reptile tanks. I use them myself and highly recommend them. However, not all lizard habitats or terrariums are constructed of glass. Herp supply manufacturers produce molded plastic and clear acrylic tanks that function both as efficient reptile containers as well as attractive display terrariums. These tanks are manufactured not only for the lizard-keepers among us, but for the herp industry as a whole, so the available variety of shapes and sizes is wide to say the least. Lastly, there are screen mesh cages that are great for chameleons and other arboreal species.

Glass Aquariums

Glass aquariums are my preferred housing option for most lizards for a number of reasons. They are widely available, come in a range of sizes and shapes, provide ventilation in the form of a screen lid, hold heat and humidity reasonable well, and—except the very large ones—are not prohibitively expensive. Most

Glass aquariums make suitable housing for many types of lizards, baby bearded dragons (*Pogona vitticeps*) in this case.

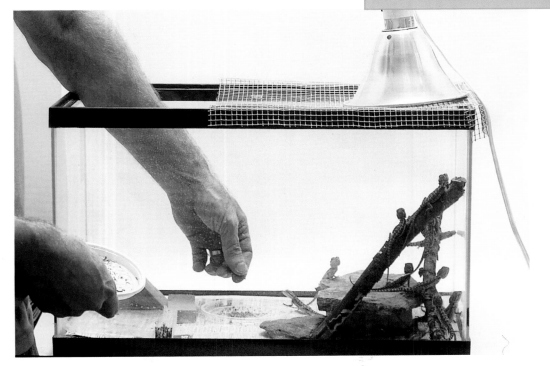

insect-eating lizards will live happily in a glass tank. However, there are a few drawbacks to glass tanks. They are somewhat fragile and are also heavy, especially in larger sizes. Large ones can be difficult to clean because you have to reach in through the top. Sometimes, it can be difficult to find the perfect combination of floor space and height that your species of lizard requires.

Some arboreal lizards, such as knight anoles (*Anolis equestris*), will thrive in tall mesh cages.

Molded Plastic and Acrylic Cages

Molded plastic cages are quite durable and attractive. Typically, they have sockets for heating and lighting built in. In most designs, three sides are opaque and one is clear glass or plastic. The glass side is also the door; these cages open from the front instead of the top. Depending on the type of lizards you keep, this can be a pro or a con. Some models are stackable, allowing you to have several in a rather small space. The major disadvantage of molded plastic tanks is the price. They are probably the most expensive housing option.

Many hobbyists favor these acrylic tanks for the numerous benefits they offer over glass. Acrylic is very durable and long lived; a direct impact or drop that would normally shatter an all-glass tank will seldom inflict any damage on an acrylic tank. Weight is also a major consideration. When constructing an elaborate, living terrarium, a hobbyist can end up constructing a very heavy environment. The combined weight of the cage materials (soil, stones, etc.) and the glass of the tank can limit a hobbyist's options for placement for the tank. Conversely, a light weight, yet sturdy acrylic tank can support the same naturalistic biome while weighing substantially less.

Acrylic tanks are not without their drawbacks, however. While most acrylics will not break like glass, many do scratch easily. A gouge or long scratch can seriously flaw the otherwise attractive face of an acrylic tank. Tiny pores in the acrylic may also become difficult to clean over time; algae or mold may become trapped in them and give the tank a stained appearance.

Cage Before Lizard

Having your terrarium already built is only half the battle when it comes to a smooth, easy transition of the lizard from the pet shop to your home; you also must have the terrarium itself up and running. This helps ensure the health and low stress levels of your new pet.

Make sure the heating apparatus for the tank is on and has been heating for a few days (after all, it may take an undertank heating pad or heating log a good while to heat the surrounding substrate), make sure that the relative humidity is already at an appropriate level, and be sure that any water dishes are filled with clean fresh water. You'll not want to feed your new acquisition for some 24 hours after bringing it home, so food isn't an issue at this point, but all other aspects of housing should be in action when the little fellow arrives. The further ahead of time the tank is set up, the more opportunity you have to notice and correct problems before your new pet is inside.

Mesh Cages

Screen mesh cages are another option. These airy enclosures ensure that species such as chameleons get sufficient air flow, and they offer climbable walls for arboreal species such as water dragons and anoles. The downside to mesh enclosures is their fragile nature. The nylon mesh of the cage is susceptible to tearing; large, heavy-bodied specimens with sharp claws (such as many species of monitor) should not be maintained in an all-mesh terrarium. In the end, glass, molded plastic, acrylic, and mesh tanks each have pros and cons; the needs of the keeper and the lizards determine which type is best.

Quarantine

The first type of terrarium that we'll discuss is the quarantine tank. The quarantine tank—which can double as a hospital tank later on should your lizards become ill—is a temporary terrarium that is meant for short-term holding and observation before you introduce your newly acquired lizard into its permanent home. Hobbyists who are planning on keeping only one lizard need not be as concerned with a quarantine tank as those hobbyists who keep multiple lizards or even a wide variety of reptile or amphibian species. The quarantine tank is your first line of defense against losing any animals in your collection. Your newly acquired animal will find it warm and comfortable, and at the first warning sign of ill health in your new specimen you'll be able to act accordingly. You and any other herps you may own will also benefit because it reduces the chance that any unnoticed disease the new lizard might have will be allowed to come into direct contact with any other herps in your collection.

Establish a quarantine tank by acquiring a terrarium of the appropriate size for the lizard. Line the bottom of the terrarium with a thick layer of white paper towels. Some hobbyists recommend using newspaper as bedding, but I must disagree with this practice. Because the ultimate goal of the quarantine tank is to allow you to monitor the health of your new pet under sterile yet hospitable conditions, newspaper makes an imperfect choice for a substrate. Newspaper, while it may work for large snake species, neither affords clawed lizards much of a gripping surface nor allows for optimum observation. If your lizard is infected with mites in quarantine, you want to be able to see the little bloodsuckers as soon as possible. On a white paper towel substrate, these tiny invaders are readily seen and treated, but when set against the multicolored backdrop of newspaper bedding, these parasites may multiply to plague proportions before you ever spot the first one. Make sure also not to use dyed, scented, or patterned paper towels, as the additional chemicals in these items, depending on the exact chemicals they contain, may be harmful to a small insectivorous lizard.

Once you have the paper towel bedding down, place some variety of sterile hideaway inside the terrarium. This hide should be small, simple, and preferably easily removed, as you may need to remove it any number of times in order to check on the health or well-being of your lizard. Excellent quarantine hides include clay flowerpot halves, plastic hide boxes (sold in most pet shops), or (in the case of arboreal geckos) slabs of

Whether you have an elaborate or simple terrarium, always have appropriate housing completely set up before acquiring your lizard.

cork bark leaned against one side of the tank. Do not place any more cover than two hide boxes for your lizards, as the whole point of quarantine is to optimize your ability to observe the quarantines animals. It is important to place one hide in the warmest portion of the tank and one in the cooler regions, so that your new lizard may enjoy the comfort and security of a hide while thermoregulating at the same time.

If you have a basking species or an arboreal species that may naturally spend a large amount of its time above the ground, such as a true chameleon or a basilisk, you'll also need to place one or more climbing branches within the quarantine terrarium. For purposes of observation, this is no problem, as a basking or arboreal species is not likely to try to hide from sight when in a comfortable terrarium environment.

Finally, place an appropriately sized water dish in the quarantine tank. Take care that this dish is neither too deep nor too steep-sided, as a great many insectivorous lizard species have adapted thin toes and finely honed sharp claws. Adapted to scale the rough surfaces of trees, rocks, and other natural structures, these claws are poorly suited for escaping up the slick sides of a ceramic, glass, or polymer watering dish. If, therefore, a small lizard were to fall into a dish that is too deep, it could easily drown in a very short amount of time. Many hobbyists avoid this scenario by placing a flat stone or short climbing branch within the water dish, such that any small lizard that might stumble into the watering dish can have a quick escape route. Always keep fresh water at your lizard's disposal. Note that some lizards may not recognize a standing bowl of water as a drinking source. These lizards will need to be misted or provided with some form of moving water, such as by aerating the water with an aquarium air pump. Regardless of how you furnish the quarantine tank, remember that it must be fitted with adequate heating and

The quarantine tank must be simple but still provide your lizard with all its needs. This is an adult bearded dragon in quarantine.

lighting apparatus. For exact heating and lighting requirements for each species, refer to the end of this chapter and to the species description section of this book.

An initial trip to the vet is always recommended after purchasing any reptile. Barring a trip to the vet, a hobbyist should look for the following signs in the quarantine tank: runny or bloody stool (a sign of internal parasites or gastrointestinal infection), tiny specks on the lizard or moving slowly around the tank (these are mites), listlessness, loss of color in the animal, vomiting, runny

Many lizards, such as the sand-swimming eastern skink (*Scincus mitratus*), have the best chance of thriving when housed in a naturalistic terrarium.

eyes, dragging limbs, encrusted vent, or any other physical symptom that suggests something is wrong with your lizard. If you suspect a health malady, visit your local veterinarian as soon as possible.

After a period of at least two or three weeks of uneventful occupation in quarantine, it's time for your lizard to move into its permanent home.

Terrarium Types

The species of lizard you own will determine just what type of terrarium you build. There are five basic types of terrariums: the rainforest/jungle tank, the desert tank, the woodland tank, the savanna tank, and the montane tank. Of course, there are variations on these five basic types, and those variations will depend on the species of lizard you have chosen to house. For example, a hobbyist keeping a sandfish skink will need to opt for fewer stones and heavy items in a desert terrarium and place more sand in the tank, as sandfish will thrive only in a tank that closely simulates the loose-sand dunes of their native Egyptian and Arabian deserts.

Each of the five basic terrarium types has its unique properties, such as substrate, humidity level, appropriate plants, etc. However, the principles of proper heating and lighting are much the same for any terrarium type. Therefore, heating and lighting are discussed in this chapter after the overviews of the terrarium types.

Space within the terrarium, whatever that terrarium style may be, is of utmost importance. Single lizard specimens obviously need less space than do colonies of lizards, though that amount of space will vary based on the species in question, so familiarize yourself with the species described later in this book before you make your purchase. Because desert and other horizontally oriented habitats will typically take up so much more room within your home than will a vertically oriented jungle habitat, limitations that you haven't banked on may enter the equation. Will you have room in your home for a 40-gallon tall terrarium? How about a 75-gallon long tank? Hit a few rooms in your house with a tape measure just to be sure that

Water in the Trees

When placing a water dish in your lizard's home, bear in mind that the species of lizard you house may or may not utilize this dish. Arboreal lizards, those species that spend a tremendous amount of time high in the treetops or in other elevated places, may drink virtually all their water from puddles and tiny pools that accumulate in the forest canopy: rain water, dew, and other condensation that collects on leaves. So if your chosen species would never seek out a pool of ground water in nature, it will not likely venture to the bottom of the terrarium to drink from a standing dish of water. Combat this problem by misting your lizard's terrarium with a handheld garden sprayer every day or every couple of days, depending on the needs of the lizard. When you mist, make sure you get plenty of droplets on the sides of the tank, the leaves of the décor, etc. After misting, watch your lizard's behavior: if it is thirsty it will very likely begin lapping up the tiny droplets with its tongue. Arboreal species that enjoy drinking water droplets include the anoles and especially the chameleons. Many geckos and some arboreal skink species also rely heavily on droplets to supply their water needs. Suspending a small dish of water high in a tall terrarium and establishing a drip-system (as is often used with chameleon species) are both excellent methods for bringing acceptable amounts of water high enough in the terrarium for your arboreal lizards to drink.

you are not biting off a bigger project than your house (or your spouse!) will allow.

Rainforest Terrarium

We'll start by looking at the rainforest or jungle terrarium. As its name suggests, this terrarium type is a hot one: high temperature, high humidity, and lots of plant cover in which your lizards can hide. The rainforest tank is a very popular terrarium style, as so many of the insectivorous lizards for sale in the pet trade today hail from these environments.

Begin by selecting an appropriately sized enclosure for the lizards you will be housing.

Example of a naturalistic rainforest terrarium suitable for day geckos, anoles, and a number of other species.

It is important to fully understand the life habits of the lizard you will be housing. Arboreal species, such as day geckos, prefer height to floor space, so those species require a tall tank. Jungle-dwelling species that live on the ground, such as ameivas, require a large floor space. If you keep such a lizard, a long and wide tank is obviously advantageous. Some lizards—basilisks, for example—need a combination of floor space and height for climbing.

In either case, heavy leaf cover is almost indispensable in the tropical terrarium, as rainforest lizards base their camouflage and survival strategies on the presence of broad leaves and thick tendrils of a jungle environment. If kept in a terrarium that is lacking in vegetative cover, these lizards will suffer stress and languish in such less-than-optimum conditions. The inability to hide or perform other natural behaviors will severely stress virtually any jungle-dwelling species.

Bear in mind, however, that the many jungle species that demand dense vegetative cover

Getting Specific

Any natural terrarium type may be tweaked by the hobbyist to mimic a very specific habitat. For example, you can control the temperature, humidity, plant life, and other parameters to accurately re-create a small slice of Costa Rican rainforest for housing your green basilisk. While creating such detailed terrariums requires painstaking research, the reward is a unique and beautiful habitat that your lizard will feel right at home in.

will also need to bask in direct sunlight. Solve this by making one side of the tank plant heavy and the other branch heavy. When the lizard needs a retreat, it will seek out the heavily planted end of the tank, but when it feels cool and needs to warm up under the rays of its basking lamp, it will readily move into the naked branches on the other side of the tank. This arrangement is much akin to how these lizards naturally live in the wild: moving into patches of sunlight when they need to be warm and moving back into shade when they want to cool off or when a threat draws near.

Humidity Although rainforests are known for their muggy atmosphere, our jungle terrariums do not need to be as moist as a hobbyist might think. In fact, a great many newcomers to the hobby make the crucial mistake of maintaining their jungle terrariums under far too moist conditions. The crux here is one of *relative humidity*; that is, the humidity that is defined as the density of water vapor that is in the air. Relative humidity is not the moisture in the soil, nor is it the puddles in the substrate or the droplets left on the walls of the terrarium after a good misting. Purchase a humidity gauge and place it inside on the middle of one of the side walls of your terrarium. Placing this gauge too near the top or the bottom of the tank may give you inaccurate readings. In a properly maintained jungle terrarium, the relative humidity should be between 65 and 80 percent. Anything above 80 percent is considered humidity saturation, and continuous exposure to such dense humidity may lead to skin and lung disorders in your pet lizards. Do not fret if the humidity levels in your terrarium do not remain constant; just as wild environments do, your jungle terrarium and its inhabitants will likely enjoy a little variation in the humidity levels.

Ventilation That variation is actually our next topic of discussion: circulation and ventilation. Unless you keep a specialized species of insectivorous lizard that requires very high and constant levels of humidity, you'll definitely want to offer adequate air circulation to your terrarium and its beasties. Air circulation keeps fresh air and high levels of oxygen inside your tank, and it helps to keep high levels of ammonia and other waste gases at a minimum. Most hobbyists can attain sufficient levels of circulation in their terrariums simply by placing a screen (metal, plastic, or nylon mesh) lid over the tank, as the screen allows for plenty of gas exchange between the terrarium and the outside environment. Covering your tank with a glass or solid acrylic lid will prevent adequate gas exchange from taking place. Unless the species you keep requires extremely high humidity, a solid plastic or glass lid will trap too much moisture in your terrarium, creating an unhealthy environment for most lizards.

Aside from a screen lid to maintain ventilation, many herp-specific terrariums come fitted with adjustable vents in their walls for ventilation. Specialized arboreal species, such as the chameleons, often require additional air circulation. Chameleons (and possibly other arboreal lizards) are probably best kept in screen cages, in which maintaining the levels of humidity can be quite difficult. Chameleon keepers often use humidifiers and/or electronic misting systems to provide for the specialized needs of their lizards. Another option—not recommended for chameleons—would be to add small vent-fans (such as those found above kitchen stoves or in bathroom ceilings) or muffin-cooling fans to a regular terrarium. This process will help to drastically increase air flow through the tank, but it will require specialized scaffolding built into the lid of the tank to support the extra weight of the fan.

A combination of live plants, a large water bowl, and the proper substrate maintain high humidity in the rainforest terrarium.

Desert Terrarium

Personally, desert terrariums are one of my favorites, as they are easily constructed and maintained, and their residents—with some exceptions—are high-

visibility lizards. Most insectivorous lizard species available in the pet trade are sun-worshippers, and they are some of the most high-visibility species you can own. There are also more secretive species—mostly geckos—that come out when the lights are off and the temperatures less burning.

Establish a desert terrarium by first selecting a tank that is appropriately sized and shaped. The same logic that governed the selection of the tropical tank is in order, but most desert-dwelling lizards have very little need for tall

Always provide desert lizards with hiding places, although many species create their own, as this curly-tail has done.

tanks or climbing branches, as their natural habitat seldom offers these items. Total floor area is the major concern where the desert species are concerned. Give these little guys plenty of room to roam about and they will thrive under your care.

Substrate After you've found an appropriately sized tank, you'll want to fill it at least 3 or 4 inches (7.6 to 10 cm) up with sand. Silica sand (like that sold for playgrounds and sandboxes) is appropriate in most cases, though granite or riverine sand can be more suitable in some instances, depending on the exact needs of your animals. Bear this general fact in mind: play sand will always be soft, smooth, and "fluid," offering minimal support to large stones or décor, while granite sand or alluvial (found in rivers) sand will pack tightly to form a semi-solid crust, which can accommodate larger or more heavy-bodied reptile species. In some instances, however, play sand is highly advantageous; the sandfish skink absolutely must be housed on loose sand if it is to live as it would in nature.

Humidity Because of the arid climate of natural deserts, it's not hard to see why any captive desert lizards we keep must have low humidity levels and a high degree of air circulation. Screen lids and very small water dishes will help to minimize humidity build-up within the terrarium. As with other things, the exact level of relative humidity at which you maintain your desert habitat will vary based on the species you keep; some lizards require far more humidity in their desert homes than do others. Place a humidity gauge on the inside in the center of one of the side walls of the terrarium to keep an eye on the humidity. A safe level of relative humidity, which should accommodate just about any species that you may purchase, is 40 to 50 percent. This is dry, but not too dry.

Many desert species require a dry terrarium with a humidified hiding area, such as one partly filled with damp sand. This mimics the way they live in the wild; their burrows are naturally more humid than the surface of the desert sands.

Hiding Places
For the most part, deserts are two things: hot and bright. There's no room for skimping when it comes to outfitting your desert terrarium with adequate heating and lighting apparatus. Be aware, however, that while your sun-loving herps need warmth and light, they also must have access to the cool and darkness that comes with deep hideaways. In fact, if it were not for a reptile's ability to escape from the blistering heat of the desert day, it would perish in a very short amount of time. Construct hides by burying broken clay pots (turned on their sides) halfway

You Are What Your Eat

Sometimes a desert lizard ingests a little bit of sand or a few small pebbles when it feeds on prey items, and, over time, these tiny bits of sediment may accumulate in the lizard's gut. This eventually causes a gut impaction. An impacted gut can be fatal for your lizard, as it blocks the colon and doesn't allow your pet to pass its meals. Preventing this condition is critical. Fortunately, an impacted gut is rare, and you can safeguard against it by sprinkling a thin layer of calcium powder along the surface of the sand in your terrarium. Herp product companies manufacture calcium-based sands that are biodegradable and will not impact your scaled friend's stomach. The drawback to these sands is that they are expensive. By sprinkling a very light dusting of calcium along the top the sand in your terrarium, you will ensure that any surface sand ingested by your lizard when it gets in a feeding frenzy will be accompanied by a minute amount of pure calcium, which will assist your lizard's gut in passing the grains of sand.

in the sandy substrate. Bury a length of PVC pipe as a hideaway for your lizards, or cement a couple of flat rocks together to form a cave into which your lizard can retreat to beat the heat. By placing hideaways in both the cooler and warmer regions of your desert terrarium, you can ensure that your animals will have the freedom to warm themselves or cool themselves as they need without their having to choose between being secure and being at the right temperature.

The Terrarium Spectrum

The remaining terrarium types can be considered variants between the two extremes of the jungle style and the desert style. For example, a woodland or temperate forest terrarium would have much higher levels of relative humidity than would a desert tank, as well as much more vegetation/climbing branches, but this terrarium would not have the high temperatures and lush, dense vegetation that we'd expect to find in a jungle tank. Similarly, a savanna or grassland style terrarium, which is suitable for a wide range of insectivorous lizards, would be much drier and more "open" than a jungle tank, but it would not be nearly as rocky or as hot as would a true desert tank. A good way to think about all terrarium types is to rank them on a continuum: the rainforest tank is on one end, the desert tank is on the other, and all other styles can be found somewhere in between. A scale descending from most moist to least moist might look something like this: jungle/rainforest, montane (like a cool jungle),

A small desert terrarium. Note the moistened sand on the right, which provides a humid burrowing area for the resident gully geckos (*Holodactylus africanus*).

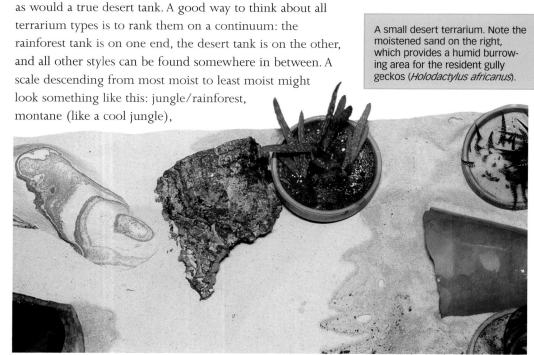

temperate forest (with live plants, but not as much daily watering as a jungle), plain/savanna/grassland (semi-moist soil, but with many dry, open areas for basking), and finally desert (least amount of moisture, and lots of bright, hot areas for basking). While any one of these terrarium types can be more or less complicated (based on the skill and determination of the hobbyist), all can be constructed, on some level of complexity, by new hobbyists.

The mountain horned dragons (*Acanthosaura* species) are among the lizards that can be housed in a montane terrarium.

Montane Terrarium

One final terrarium style that I want to discuss in some depth, and which you might not logically think to place on the continuum between the desert and the jungle habitats, is the montane-style terrarium. Montane means "mountainous," and a montane-style terrarium can house high altitude-dwelling lizard species. Several relatively common lizards hail from mountainous habitats, including mountain horned dragons, several chameleon species, and, of course, the dazzling but delicate emerald swift. Most of the montane lizards in the pet trade come from the mountains of China and other parts of Asia.

Begin constructing a montane habitat with an equal balance of height and floor space in mind, because many montane species both climb and wander the cage floor. Montane lizards, with some exceptions, also relish thick vegetative cover, so make sure to include plenty of leafy cover and dark hideaways. Climbing branches are essential, as is a basking spot, though the heat supplied in this basking spot need not be as warm as that in the jungle tank. And that is just where the montane habitat is unique: it is typically much cooler than any other terrarium style.

Temperature and Humidity Because of the high elevation, the montane environment is much cooler than the surrounding lowlands and jungles. To help maintain a cooler environment in the terrarium, consider placing the terrarium in one of the cooler rooms in your house, such as a basement or ground-level bedroom. To minimize excess heat, you should employ a fluorescent light bulb to illuminate the tank instead of an incandescent one, as the fluorescent bulb will emit far less heat than its incandescent counterpart. As is true of all aspects of reptile keeping, a solid understanding of the exact needs of your chosen species is critical to the success of your insectivorous lizard endeavor. Some montane lizards need a cool terrarium with a warmer basking site. For these species, it is best to use a large tank with a basking spot lamp as far to one end as possible. Most montane species need a significant temperature drop at night. I am hesitant to list exact temperature parameters for this terrarium type, as certain species' needs can vary greatly from others. All hobbyists are encouraged to meet the specific requirements of their chosen species. Suffice it to say that basking temperatures rarely need to exceed the low 80s (26.7-28.3°C) and lows may dip into the mid 60s (17.8-18.9°C) at night.

When it comes to humidity, you should follow very closely the guidelines established for the jungle terrarium. The montane lizards found in the pet trade are from high elevation forests that are shrouded in cool fog and settled in heavy dews. These lizards require a high level of relative humidity, usually 65 to 75 percent. High levels of air circulation are also mandatory: employ a screen lid with plenty of ventilation.

Non-Naturalistic Terrariums

Although natural terrariums are beautiful and allow captive lizards the greatest opportunity to perform natural behaviors, not every keeper has the inclination or resources to create such elaborate setups. Luckily, most insectivorous lizard species can thrive under less complicated conditions. By supplying more vegetation and hiding locales, the Spartan quarantine tank can function as permanent housing for your lizards. While not as visually stunning, a scantly decorated tank can successfully house almost any species, just so long as the humidity, lighting, and heating needs of the species are met. Professional breeders and hobbyists with large collections typically prefer to house their insectivorous lizards as cheaply and as practically as possible, although most will also maintain a more lavishly decorated show tank. It's not out of the question for you too to house your pets in a more simplistic enclosure. Just research your chosen species and make sure that your terrarium—whatever style you choose to build—meets all of that species's needs.

Heating and Lighting

Reptiles and amphibians are cold-blooded, or ectothermic as some folks like to say. This means that reptiles and amphibians do not produce their own body heat and therefore must soak in all necessary heat from their surroundings. And lizards need heat to move, to feed, and to metabolize their meals.

Only use heat rocks with a reliable thermostat to prevent your lizard (a panther gecko in this photo) from burning itself.

Because lizards cannot sweat or pant to rid themselves of excess heat, they must be able to come and go from areas of higher heat to areas of lesser heat. This is called behavioral thermoregulation; when a lizard is cool early in the morning, it will crawl into the sun to bask and raise its temperature. When it reaches its optimum temperature, the lizard will scuttle off to catch insects and live its daily life. If during the course of the day the lizard gets too hot, it must retreat into a cool, shady area in order to cool down; remember, an overheated lizard that cannot find a cooler retreat will die. Nocturnal lizards will often warm themselves by resting on a branch or stone that has absorbed the heat of the sun, moving off to feed or mate when they have reached their preferred temperature.

Create a thermal gradient in your terrarium by heating one end more than the other. A basking light suspended above a large rock, for example, would make a hotter basking spot for your lizard, while a dark cave at the other end of the tank would make an excellent retreat in which your lizard could escape the heat and cool down. High ventilation (i.e., screen lids and ventilation fans) helps to keep air temperatures within the terrarium from spiking to unacceptably high levels. Never place a terrarium in a sunny window, as the entire tank can heat to lethal levels in a surprisingly short amount of time.

Heating Equipment

In captivity, hobbyists can supply heat and light to their pets in a number of ways, though the exact types of heating and lighting apparatus you'll need will vary depending on what species of lizard you house. Let's start by discussing heating apparatus.

Direct-Contact Heating Direct-contact heating items are placed inside the lizard's enclosure and have cords that run out through the lid of the tank and plug into the wall. Constructed of ceramics or resin surrounding an internal heating coil, these items work on the same principle as a heating blanket. The lizard may sit atop the hot item until reaching its desired temperature and then may scuttle off when it gets too hot. This allows the lizard to thermoregulate itself easily. These heating items are also aesthetically attractive. Often molded into logs, cattle skulls, caves, or tree stumps, they are diverse enough to function while looking attractive in virtually any terrarium style that you might establish.

On the downside, however, is that these items pose a potential health hazard to your animals. Heating decorations are sometimes constructed with imperfections. The coil inside may get too hot, or the resin covering the heating coil may be too thin in spots, or the item's cord may be poorly connected. The result of any one of these scenarios is that your lizard may be severely burned or electrocuted upon making contact with the heating item. Today's heating decorations are well manufactured, and such catastrophes are rare. I do, however, caution against any scenario that will allow your insectivorous lizard to burrow beneath any type of heating apparatus, as this can lead to the animal's becoming trapped and quickly overheating to the point of death.

Another drawback to using the in-tank heating décor items is that their cord must leave the tank somehow. If this creates a hole or gap between the tank and its lid, then that is a possible escape route for most types of lizards. Do not compromise the security of your terrarium! Lastly, it is not wise for you to use one of these items as the only heating device in the terrarium. This creates a situation in which your lizard must stay on the rock

Provide your lizard with a range of temperatures in the terrarium so it can control its own body temperature. A checkered whiptail (*Cnemidophorus tesselatus*) is shown here.

to maintain its temperature, which can cause burns on the belly and inability to perform normal behaviors because the lizard must spend all of its time on the rock.

Heat emitters are useful for providing heat to nocturnal species, such as Bibron's gecko (*Pachydactylus bibronii*)

Undertank Heating Pads

The next type of heating gear is one that hobbyists far and wide swear by: the undertank heating pad. Manufactured by a wide range of herp-care companies, these little gadgets have definitely got some advantages. Begin by unpacking the pad and removing the film from the adhesive side. Position the pad under the tank—or on the wall in the case of arboreal geckos—on the outside of the glass. Make sure you position it well, because once you stick it on, it cannot be removed and safely repositioned (without risking damage to internal components). These pads then plug into the wall to offer even, gentle radiant warmth to your herps, and they present virtually none of the risks of in-tank style heating decorations.

One drawback I have noted, however, is that lizard species that require thicker substrate may not benefit from an undertank heating pad, as very little warmth can penetrate upward through the layers of substrate. When a heating pad goes foul (cords rip, internal heating coil dies, etc.) after a number of years, it can be incredibly difficult to remove the pad and dispose of it. Placing a replacement pad in exactly the same spot may not work well, either, as the contact between old glue and the new may cause the new not to stick so solidly. In short, the placement of an undertank heating pad is, by and large, a "for-keeps" kind of deal.

Heat Emitters The final type of heating apparatus is the ceramic heat emitter. Let me begin by saying that this thing gets hot! Designed for use in large terrariums (where large areas of land and air must be heated), ceramic heat emitters are coils of heating wire encased in a ceramic bulb-like structure; they are made to be used with high-heat resistant, ceramic fixtures only; standard department store dome lights will melt and burn when used with a ceramic heat emitter. Use only approved equipment with these high-heat items.

Heat emitters are useful to the hobbyist who has to heat a very large desert or savanna environment, or even perhaps a large jungle terrarium, though any plant life that is placed too near this item will certainly die. Because heat emitters produce heat without producing light, they are excellent for heating a terrarium at night. Never place heat emitters too close to the glass walls of your tank, as there is a chance that the glass will shatter under the intense heat. If you do have call to use a heat emitter, make sure it is kept at a safe distance away from your pets; many hobbyists choose to hang these emitters from a drop-cord suspended from the ceiling so that heat can gently radiate downwards into the tank.

Lighting

Lighting in the captive terrarium is extremely important to many lizard species. Lizards, like many other reptiles, require a certain amount of exposure to the invisible ultraviolet (UV) radiation found in the sun's natural, unfiltered light. The two types of UV light that hobbyists need to understand are referred to as UVA and UVB. Both of these are critical to the long-term survival of diurnal lizards. Most diurnal lizards need UV radiation for their bodies to properly develop musculature and bone structure, as well as for the same emotional benefits that we as humans derive from sunlight. While lizard emotions are not remotely as complex as our own, they are surprisingly sophisticated, and ample daily exposure to UV radiation will keep stress levels down and stimulate natural behaviors. UVA and UVB may be obtained in one of two ways: from natural sunlight or from specialized light bulbs (usually called full-spectrum bulbs).

Undertank heaters are useful for many species that would not appreciate bright basking lights, such as leopard geckos (*Eublepharis macularius*).

Natural Sunlight You may construct for your pets an outdoor terrarium that gives them access to unfiltered (no glass or plastic ceilings) sunlight. This is often very expensive, and in many parts of the world it is impractical for the average lizard hobbyist to take his or her pet outside for several hours each day, as winter gets intolerably cold. If you have the opportunity to take your lizard outside safely (guarding against escapes or attacks by cats, dogs, etc.) it is highly recommended, as your little scaled friend (with the exception of nocturnal species, such as most geckos) will

Natural sunlight is the best type of lighting for your lizard. A basking green anole (*Anolis carolinensis*) is shown here.

definitely enjoy catching some natural rays. Make sure your lizard has the opportunity to move out of the light and cool off. Otherwise, it may fatally overheat.

Full-Spectrum Light Bulbs The next best thing to actual sunlight is artificial sunlight, which comes in the form of special light bulbs sold at your local pet shop. Manufactured for either incandescent or fluorescent fixtures, these full-spectrum light bulbs are made to simulate varying degrees of sunlight and UV radiation. For example, a full-spectrum bulb that offers UVA and UVB of 2 percent would be suitable for most forest and jungle species, as those species often stay deep under forest canopies, so the most intense light of day may only trickle down to them on the forest floor. Desert and savanna-going species, however, may spend much more of their time directly in the sun, so bulbs offering UVA and UVB of 5 or 10 percent are in order. Make sure you know the specific behavior of your animal before purchasing a UV bulb; you don't want to give your pet too much or too little UV radiation. Any species that basks for long periods probably needs the higher amounts of UV light. The incandescent full-spectrum lights often emit substantial heat along with the UV.

It's important that the bulb be close enough to the lizard that your pet gets the full benefits of the UV. UV radiation scatters and dissipates once it gets several inches (10 cm or more) from the bulb. Most fluorescent bulbs provide UV within 12 inches (30.5 cm) of the bulb, while most of the full-spectrum incandescent lights emit UV to a distance of 18-24 inches (45.7-61 cm). Angle your basking rocks and branches so that your lizards can get within this distance from the light. Also note that glass and plastic absorb UV light, so there should be nothing more than screening between your lizard and the bulb.

Other Lights Other types of lighting include standard incandescent and standard fluorescent bulbs that may be found in home fixtures. These bulbs can be employed in the insectivorous lizard terrarium for illumination and heating purposes only. While they allow you to see clearly inside the tank, no amount of regular fluorescent or incandescent lighting will give your lizard the necessary amount of UV radiation it needs. Incandescent bulbs can be used to maintain the temperature of the terrarium in the proper range and provide a hot spot for basking.

A final type of lighting is the night-cycle bulb. Night-cycle bulbs are light bulbs that are very low wattage and are often constructed with red or blue glass (the blue ones are sometimes referred to as "moonglow" bulbs). These bulbs are turned on only at night to afford extra heat to the terrarium without an intrusive amount of light. Many nocturnal species (such as tokays and other arboreal geckos) can be successfully observed at night by using these bulbs. The leopard geckos and their allies can also benefit greatly, especially during breeding season, through the use of night-cycle bulbs.

Substrates

Bearded dragons and many other day-active desert lizards require both heat lamps and full-spectrum lights for good health.

As you've already seen in our earlier discussion of the desert terrarium, "substrate" is a general term for any sort of

ground cover or bedding that you use on the bottom of your lizard's enclosure. Some hobbyists who prefer ease of maintenance over naturalistic or aesthetic appearance may use folded newspapers or paper towels to cover the bottom of the tank, while hobbyists who enjoy both the natural beauty and challenges presented by a naturalistic terrarium may place several layers of biologically active soil, peat, mulch, or other organic matter in which living plants will thrive; such an elaborate tank is also known as a vivarium.

Choosing the right substrate for your tank is an important step in ensuring a successful and long-lived endeavor. Make sure you know all the basic needs and care information for your chosen species of lizard before you begin construction of its terrarium. If you have decided to keep some manner of jungle lizard, then a substrate that holds moisture is in order; many pet shops sell pre-packaged bags of "jungle mix" substrate, which can simply be poured into the terrarium. These bags of mix are very convenient for beginning hobbyists, and I highly recommend them. If, however, you have decided upon some manner of desert–dwelling lizard, then a sandy or rocky substrate will definitely be in order. Again, the herp industry can provide you with bagged sands (either the inorganic variety or the manufactured calcium-sand, which is fully digestible should your pet accidentally ingest any of it) that can make terrarium construction very easy. In all aspects of lizard keeping, knowledge is power, and the more knowledge you have about the biological parameters and requirements of your lizard, the more well equipped you will be in meeting those needs. Cedar, pine, and aspen shavings are inappropriate substrates for almost all lizards, and you should not use them.

UV Half-Life

Normally we would never replace a light bulb in our house until it went out, right? It would be silly to replace a bulb that was still burning and lighting a room. But UV bulbs are simply not that way; these bulbs decompose over time: they lose some of their UV output capabilities long before they actually burn out. So it is possible for your lizard to not be getting enough UV radiation, despite the fact that its UV lamp is still burning strongly. Most hobbyists agree that after six months of life, fluorescent UV bulbs tend to start breaking down in efficiency. After six months, it's time to replace those bulbs. Incandescent UV bulbs last for several years, a fact that justifies their higher price.

Chapter 3

Food and Feeding

Every keeper of every age and experience level loves feeding time in the insectivorous lizard terrarium, as this is the time when we get to see our little pals in action. And because so many species of insectivorous lizards are hearty eaters, the captive diet seldom presents a problem. But there are a number of things to to keep in mind when sitting your lizard down at the dinner table.

Variety

The cardinal rule to keep in mind at feeding time is that variety is the key to keeping your lizard healthy, happy, and not bored! It may sound odd, but a lizard (especially a chameleon) can become bored and uninterested in its food if you offer it the same fare day after day after day. Mix it up to keep your lizard darting and dashing after its next prey item. Offer crickets once a week, then offer a couple of hefty mealworms at the next feeding, then, maybe, jazz it up by presenting your scaled pal with a few fat, juicy wax worms. You can find many types of feeder insects by searching the Internet, pet stores, and herp expos. Besides preventing boredom, offering a wide variety of insects helps to make sure your lizard receives all the vitamins and minerals it needs in order to live long and thrive. It's fine to use crickets or mealworms as a staple, but it's important to include other items in the diet.

Gut-Loading and Supplements

Gut-loading is one of most important diet-related concepts to understand when you are keeping insect-eating lizards. Building on the age-old premise that "you are what you eat," gut-loading is the technique of feeding high-quality food items to the feeder organisms that you will offer to your lizard. Feeder insect suppliers often feed their livestock a nutrient-poor diet. As a result, the lizards that consume these nutrient-poor feeders take in only a minimal amount of

In nature, most lizards feed on a variety of prey. This wild armadillo lizard (*Cordylus ukingensis*) is feeding on a grasshopper.

vitamins, minerals, and other nutrients. By keeping your feeder bugs for a day or two and making sure that they feed on nutritious fare, you can ensure that they are full of vital nutrients they will pass on to your lizard!

While many experts recommend gut-loading your prey items on dry dog food, cereal, and other grain mixtures, I have found that fish flakes work best for transferring nutrients from the feeder to the predator. And because mealworms and crickets are typically always hungry, gut-loading is very easy. Simply dump some fish food flakes into a container with the prey items and let them eat for 24 to 48 hours before offering them to your lizards. Be aware, however, that some types of feeders will not eat this food. Wax worms, silkworms, and flies have more specialized diets and need to be fed a different diet.

Supplements

While gut-loading will meet most of our lizard friends' nutritional needs, there are still some vital nutrients that must be added to their diet by using vitamin and mineral supplements. Supplements are added to the diet by dusting the feeder bugs. Dusting is the practice of placing a few feeders into a small container, sprinkling a little vitamin and calcium powder in, gently shaking it up such that the powders cling to the insects, and feeding the coated insects to your lizards. While it sounds simple enough, there are a few rules to bear in mind when dusting your feeders insects.

One of the main questions that comes up in dusting is "How much is enough?" You don't need to thickly coat these feeder items; a light dusting is always sufficient. In the end, your prey items should come away with a pale appearance. The next question is one of frequency: "How often do I dust feeders?" This question can only truly be answered at the species level. Each lizard species will have different requirements, as will juveniles versus their adult counterparts. The best general advice I can offer is to

You can feed wild insects to increase the variety you offer your pet lizards.

dust with calcium powder at least twice as often as you dust with vitamin meal. Calcium is integral to the proper muscular, endocrine, and skeletal development of growing lizards, and, since most lizard species grow throughout the duration of their lives, they constantly need these nutrients. If given in excess, the unused calcium simply passes out of your lizard through its urine and feces. Vitamin powder, however, should be used more sparingly, as a multivitamin mixture can lead to toxicity; juveniles of all species are particularly at risk because of their small body mass. Vitamin A is an example of a vitamin that does not leave the body very quickly, so if high levels of it are given as a supplement in each meal, then it will not be long before such vitamins begin to over-accumulate in your pet's system.

When it comes to selecting a particular vitamin supplement, make sure you know all you can about your chosen species. Some lizards need more or less of certain vitamins, while other species may require slightly different vitamin ratios. All in all, however, most insectivorous species will have their needs met by a wide-spectrum supplement. Several brands of wide-spectrum supplement are available through any pet shop that carries herps. A good rule of thumb is to purchase a supplement that has moderate amounts of vitamin A in it; compare the labels on a few bottles if you are uncertain. Also, the best supplements separate the vitamins from minerals. This is because minerals can cause the vitamins to decompose. You should plan on purchasing one vitamin supplement and one calcium and mineral supplement.

Wax worms are high in fat, making them a good item to feed sick or underweight lizards.

Feeding Frequency

A final aspect of feeding is frequency. Since feeding time is a time when we truly get to interact with our lizards, hobbyists tend to feed too often. This is not a good thing, as, just as is true of humans, lizards can grow obese.

The good news is that insectivorous lizards have relatively higher metabolisms than large carnivorous species such as monitors and tegus, so they don't tend to get overweight so fast. That's not to say it can't happen, however. Some good guidelines to follow are that baby lizards (hatchlings and neonates) need to eat as often as possible, preferably two to three times per day. Once they start to fill out and get a little more weight, you can ease the feeding frequencies back to once per day, then once every two days. Adult lizards of most species should be fed at a frequency of once (with several feeders per each feeding) every two to three days. Only under special circumstances, such as an in the case of an underweight or actively breeding individual, should an adult be fed more frequently than that.

Feeder Insects

Now that you know some of the feeding basics, let's take a look at just what is on the menu.

Crickets

Crickets, almost invariably, are the most commonly sold feeder insects in the industry today. These six-legged chirpers are rich in protein and are very easy to gut-load and maintain for a brief period of time. Their movements often lure even picky lizards into eating. The only drawback to feeding too many crickets is that if your lizard has no interest in feeding on them, the insects will be left to roam about the terrarium, often climbing atop or even nibbling upon your pet lizard. Free-ranging crickets can be a major source of

Size Does Matter

When it comes to offering prey items to your insectivorous lizards, size truly does matter. A large lizard may completely disregard the pinhead crickets you offer, and a baby bearded dragon would be overwhelmed by a writhing king mealworm. A good rule of thumb is to offer your pet a feeder item that is roughly one-third the size of the pet's head.

Just bear in mind that if it takes your lizard a lot of time and effort to consume one feeder item, you'll probably want to decrease the size of the feeders you're offering. Feeding oversized prey can cause a host of problems, perhaps the worst of which are gastrointestinal problems. In short, always feed your lizard prey items that look as though they can easily fit into the lizard's mouth. Prey items that are too small may go uneaten, and those that are too large may injure your lizard upon consumption.

discomfort and stress to an uninterested lizard. If your lizard does not show interest in live crickets after a few minutes, remove them from the terrarium and try again later. Give your lizards the number of crickets it can eat in 10 minutes or so and remove any left over.

Mealworms

Mealworms are also a common— and excellent— prey item to offer to your lizards. Actually the larval form of a beetle (*Tenebrio molitor*, one of the darkling beetles), this wriggly little critter isn't a true worm. Mealworms, while easily gut-loaded, have powerful mandibles, and large specimens can inflict painful, damaging bites on very small and delicate lizards. Make sure you feed appropriately sized fare to your pets, as an overly large mealworm is entirely inappropriate for a small or juvenile lizard. Mealworms may be kept in containers for months at a time. If kept above 45°F (7.2°C), they will metamorphose into small beetles, which many lizards will also eagerly devour. To avoid metamorphosis, store these worms in a refrigerated environment that does not rise above 45°F (7.2°C). When kept at room temperature and with nutritious food, the beetles will readily breed. This will supply you with a steady supply of mealworms at a variety of sizes. Additionally, you can hunt through the colony for white mealworms. These are mealworms that have freshly shed their old exoskeletons. They are more easily digested than regular mealworms and are useful for feeding to sick lizards and delicate species, as well as for coaxing reluctant feeders.

Flightless fruit flies are sold in colonies that last about two weeks. Never feed your lizards flies from moldy colonies.

King Mealworms

As though they are the bigger brothers of the regular mealworms, king mealworms (also called super mealworms) are easily two or three times the size of standard mealworms. They are a different species, *Zophobas morio*. While they offer considerably more nutrients, they can also inflict far more damage with their powerful mandibles. For larger lizards, such as bearded dragons, basilisks, and water dragons, they are a fantastic feeder. Use caution feeding these larval insects to smaller lizards, however.

Do not store king mealworms at or below 55°F (12.8°C). King mealworms have a more specialized life cycle than regular mealworms, so it is much more difficult to raise them as a colony.

Wax Worms

Wax worms are grub-like white caterpillars that turn into a common wax moth (*Galleria melonella*). They are small, plump, and perfectly defenseless, making them seemingly the ideal feeder. However, wax worms do not feed on commonly available gut-loading material, so it is not possible to gut-load them. Wax worms are high in fat but offer little in the way of other nutrients. Offer them occasionally or use them to put weight on a thin or sickly lizard.

Finicky eaters also may take wax worms before accepting other prey. The adult wax moths themselves are also tempting to many lizards.

Other "Worms"

There are a number of other larval insects sold as feeders. These include silkworms, tomato hornworms, butter worms, and others. These alternative feeders are available from specialized suppliers that you can locate online or at herp expos. Silkworms—the larvae of the silk moth—are extremely nutritious and can be your staple food item, if you wish. The drawback to them is that they are relatively expensive. Both silkworms and tomato hornworms require specialized diets that are available from the same suppliers as the worms themselves. These two

Although they are expensive, silkworms are one of the most nutritious insects you can feed to your lizards.

worms can get rather large, making them a good choice for some of the larger lizards, such as bearded dragons, basilisks, and water dragons.

Flightless Fruit Flies

Flightless fruit flies (bred to have stunted wings) are available as colonies in tiny cylinders or larger ones in quart-sized (liter-sized) containers. The breeding and feeding medium is a gel or liquid high in nutrients. Two species are available, one a bit larger than the other, but both species are tiny. Only the smallest of lizards will be interested in taking fruit flies. If you have purchased a very young lizard, or if your lizard has lain eggs and those eggs are soon to hatch and you'll need something on which to rear the hatchlings, then fruit flies may be just the thing for you.

Flies and Maggots

Maggots are in fact very nutritious items. Available through specialized pet shops and online reptile sites, maggots may be fed to your insectivorous lizards in all three stages of their life cycle: the larva (the maggot itself), the pupa, and the adult fly. Recently, feeders

Going Native

Some hobbyists like to save money and a trip to the pet shop by catching wild insects and other invertebrates as prey items for their pets. It also greatly increases the variety of food your pet is eating. While this can be a good idea, it can also have some serious negative consequences. First and foremost, make sure that you are not collecting these wild prey items from an area (such as a park or farm) that has been treated with pesticides, herbicides, or other chemicals. Many pesticides and herbicides may contaminate insect life long before killing them, so simply because your tube of grasshoppers is alive and kicking now doesn't mean that they aren't contaminated with something that could be harmful to your lizard upon ingestion. A second major consideration is the type of insect you offer. Brightly colored insects, such as ladybugs, are often protected by a foul taste or internal poisons, while hairy or wooly caterpillars often wear a chemical defense system of venomous or irritating spines and hairs. If you are going to feed wild bugs, it's best to become familiar with any harmful ones that are found in your area.

called Phoenix worms have become available. These "worms" are the larval stage of the black soldier fly (*Hermetia illucens*), so they are technically maggots. They are excellent high-calcium feeders. You can find them online, at herp expos, and at reptile-oriented pet stores.

Roaches

While the notion of using roaches as feeder items may sound deeply unappealing at first, bear in mind that you won't be feeding the scum-eating, street-prowling, filthy type of roaches found in gutters and rubbish piles. You'll be feeding farm-raised roaches that have been fed on fruits and other high-quality foods. The most commonly available species of roaches include Madagascar hissing

Tomato hornworms are now commercially available. They get large quickly making them a good choice for feeding big lizards.

roaches (*Gromphradorhina portentosa*), lobster roaches (*Nauphoeta cinerea*), orange-headed roaches (*Eublaberus prosticus*), death's head roaches (*Blaberus craniifer*), Guyana orange-spot roaches (*Blaptica dubia*), six-spot roaches (*Eublaberus distanti*), and Cuban green roaches (*Panchlora nivea*).

All of these species are tropical, and they will not thrive in or infest your home should any escape. Because some of these species can thrive in extreme southern Florida, Florida state law forbids the import of sale of these species. Always check local and state laws before importing exotic prey items. While it wouldn't do to release a crop of these roaches in your house, as feeders they make excellent additions to any lizard menu. Several species can climb up glass, which makes preventing escapes a bit tricky. A 2-inch wide (5 cm) band of petroleum jelly across the top edge of the tank walls combined with a fine mesh screen lid will keep the roaches in the cage until you are ready to feed them to your lizards.

Roaches have a shelf life that may exceed several months, which allows for extended periods of gut-loading; you simply cannot get this same amount of gut-loading with any other feeder insects. Several of the species also breed readily, creating a steady supply of these nutritious feeders at different sizes. Simply house your roaches in a small terrarium of their own with newsprint or mulch bedding and a varied diet of fruit, vegetables, and tropical fish flake food until you are ready to offer them to your lizards.

Mice and Other Vertebrates

Larger insectivorous lizards frequently prey on small vertebrates in the wild. Depending on the species of lizard and habitat, these prey items might include other lizards, fish, frogs, snakes, nestling birds, and rodents and other small mammals. If you keep one of these larger lizards, you can offer them some of those items. Some species that may eat vertebrates include bearded dragons, water dragons,

Insects in a Can

Most pet stores that offer reptiles or amphibians also offer freeze-dried insects. There are also canned snails and earthworms for those species that will eat them. Sold in cans or small bottles, these freeze-dried insects are safely preserved with virtually all of their nutrients intact. Needless to say, their shelf-life is very long indeed. Most insectivorous lizards can gradually be weaned into accepting freeze-dried insects. Simply offer some freeze-dried insects at the same time and in the same part of the terrarium in which you offer live fare. Over time, offer more preserved items and fewer live ones during those times that you wish to alter your pet's diet such that it gets more preserved insects. Several companies also make vibrating food dishes that give vigorous movement to the otherwise stationary preserved insects. I do not recommend feeding any species of insectivorous lizard a diet of preserved insects exclusively.

basilisks, and Sudan plated lizards. Because of the risk of transferring parasites to your lizards, it is best to avoid feeding them other reptiles, amphibians, or wild birds and rodents. If you feed large insectivorous lizards fish, it is best to freeze the fish first to help reduce the risk of passing along parasites.

The best vertebrates to feed are domestically raised mice and chicks. You can buy these prey items frozen or live. It is more convenient, more humane, and safer to feed frozen mice and chicks, but many insect-eating lizards won't eat prey that doesn't move.

You can try wiggling the prey with forceps, but this may not fool your lizard into thinking that soggy mouse is food. For these lizards, live is the only option.

Allow frozen mice or chicks to defrost to room temperature slowly. Do not thaw them in a microwave oven—the results can be very messy! You can also defrost them more quickly by placing them in a sandwich bag and immersing the bag in warm water. Feed rodents and chicks that are an appropriate size for your lizard; follow the same guidelines as if you were feeding crickets. The lizards in this book that can eat small vertebrates usually will eat pinkie mice (hairless newborns) or fuzzy mice (newborns that have just grown their hair), not adult mice.

Because vertebrates are higher in fat than insects and because none of the species included in this book feed mainly on vertebrates, do not feed your lizard mice or chicks more than once or twice a month. If you have a lizard that is underweight, you can feed a few pinkies each week

You can feed adult green basilisks (*Basiliscus plumifrons*) and other large lizards baby mice on occasion.

Chapter 4

Health Care

As much as I hate to admit it, there is a downside to keeping insectivorous lizards. Our little friends can get burned on heating apparatus. They may fall and break a limb. Extended periods of improper diet and lighting can lead to crippling ailments. And there are very many internal and external parasites out there just waiting to feed on the vital fluids of our scaly pets. That's the bad news. The good news is that a little knowledge and some competency at husbandry practices on the part of the keeper are typically all it takes to thwart each and every one of these ailments before they ever take hold of our lizards. Prevention is critical to never needing a cure. By providing your animals with the proper habitat conditions and proper nutrition, and by following safety guidelines when handling your lizard, you can go a long way in preventing disaster from ever striking you and your captives.

The Veterinarian

The first thing to consider when it comes to the long-term health of your pet lizards is the availability of a reptile-specific veterinarian. Is there a vet in your town who deals with herps or is specifically trained in the diseases and disorders of exotic reptiles? Try asking around your local pet shops or searching online to find the nearest vet. It is absolutely necessary to locate a reptile-specific vet *before* a problem arises with your pet. It is also a good idea to take your lizard to a reptile vet soon after you acquire it to check for parasites or assess the general health of your new pet.

Quarantine First

Begin treatment of all ailments by moving your animal to a quarantine tank as described in the housing chapter. This can help prevent the problem from spreading to other lizards and will allow you to keep a closer eye on the sick lizard.

External Parasites

Perhaps the most common affliction found in recently purchased lizards (especially wild-caught individuals) are external parasites. External parasites appear in two forms: ticks and mites. These organisms are related to each other—both are arachnids in the order Acarina—and both feed on blood. However, they have a number of differences and require different treatment

Ticks

Ticks are small, flat, and reddish to gray in color; they may be seen crawling on—or, more frequently, attached to— your lizard. You will normally find them on the head (usually around the eyes, ears, and throat) or cloaca of your lizard. Ticks feed by embedding themselves between the scales of your lizard and biting through the interstitial skin beneath; their sharp mandibles break the skin and feed on the blood that oozes forth.

Treat ticks by swabbing them with rubbing alcohol, waiting about 10 minutes, then gently pulling them off with a pair of tweezers. If the parasite remains alive, drop it into a small container of the alcohol and dispose of it when it's dead. Bear in mind that if your animal has a dense infestation of ticks, and removing them all at once would leave a serious wound or would be overly traumatic for the lizard, you shouldn't remove all the ticks in one sitting. Swab them with alcohol, and remove a few every day until they are all gone.

Mites

Mites are the second, and, sadly, more common type of the external parasites that afflict insect-eating lizards. Appearing as tiny red, black, or gray flecks, these minuscule blood-suckers are very tiny, like living grains of sand. They feed in the same way as ticks and congregate around the eyes, ears, armpits, cloaca, mouth, and nostrils of their hosts, for these are areas where the skin is thin and the number of blood-filled capillaries is high. Check for the presence of mites by wetting a white paper towel and scrubbing your lizard gently. Inspect the paper towel. Do you see slowly moving flecks? If you do, then it's time to kill some mites!

Your mode of attack will largely depend on what type of lizard you house. When treating mite infestations in geckos and other lizards with very fine, non-overlapping scales, you need only bathe the lizard with clean lukewarm water and gently brush away all visible mites. With no overlapping scales under which they can hide, the mites will be flushed down the drain. If, however, you have a lizard whose scales overlap (and this is most species you'll encounter), you'll have to repeat this washing process daily until all mites disappear. When treating heavily scaled species, such as the swifts and the sungazers, it may be helpful to use a toothpick or cotton swab to gently pick under the scales and root out any hiding mites.

Because mites are so insidious and can quickly and easy spread from tank to tank to infect an entire reptile collection, any infected specimens must be moved into another room of the house *immediately*. All substrate and living decorations (vegetation of all types) must be disposed of, and all inorganic materials, including the tank itself, must be washed thoroughly in hot soapy water in order to kill any remaining mites or their eggs. Mite

Tick on the leg of a wild-caught monitor. Captive-bred lizards rarely carry ticks.

eggs are very tough and may survive this treatment; be prepared to wash out the tank several times.

You can also get mite treatments from your vet. This is usually the drug ivermectin. This is misted onto the lizard and tank as per your vet's instructions. This is a very safe and effective treatment. The only caution is that ivermectin is toxic to turtles and tortoises, so be very careful with this drug if you keep those reptiles as well as lizards.

Internal Parasites

Of course, not all parasites are external. A wide variety of parasites may infest the gastrointestinal tract of lizards. This is primarily a problem seen in wild-caught lizards, but captive-bred animals can also contract parasites from infested lizards. While pinworms and hookworms are the most dangerous to your pets (because they have a complete life-cycle within your lizard and can reproduce to fatal levels inside your pet), other nematodes, flatworms, flukes, and other invertebrate vermin can all present a wide variety of problems. This is where a relative inexpensive diagnostic trip to the vet is in order. Because it can be very difficult for even highly experienced herpetologists to properly identify and treat internal parasites, I cannot recommend that identification and treatment be conducted by the average enthusiast, as misdiagnosis and an unskilled hand at treatment can easily lead to the death of your pet.

If your pet suffers from any of the following symptoms, an internal parasite infestation may be the cause, and a diagnostic veterinarian check-up is in order:

• Runny or bloody stool
• Sudden loss of appetite and loss of weight
• Increased appetite coupled with loss of weight
• Vomiting
• Worms or their eggs visible in stool

Wild-caught lizards frequently have mites, shown here on a crevice spiny lizard (*Sceloporus poinsettii*).

Internal parasites are typically treated by oral medications, although injectable drugs are sometimes used. Many times, reptiles will have low levels of parasites that cause no problems until the animal suffers from prolonged stress that weakens the immune system. Proper husbandry often prevents these parasites from becoming a problem.

Keeping Everybody Healthy

Maintaining a clean facility that is free of feces and urine build-up is essential in curbing the spread of bacteria of the genus *Salmonella*, **which live in the digestive tracts of most reptiles. These bacteria can cause a severe infection in people if they get into our eyes, mouth, or open wounds.**

The daily observance of simple rules of hygiene is all it takes to prevent the spread of salmonellosis. Here are some guidelines to follow:

- **Never let children handle a lizard unsupervised; make sure they understand to never put their hands near their eyes, nose, or mouth during or after handling a lizard.**
- **Do not eat, drink, or smoke when handling your lizard or servicing the cage.**
- **Always wash your hands with antibacterial soap immediately after handling a lizard.**
- **Never allow your animals to walk across kitchen countertops, tables, or other areas where human food preparation occurs.**
- **Never allow your lizard to crawl over your face or inside your mouth.**

Respiratory Infections

Respiratory ailments are typically brought about by improper levels of humidity in the terrarium environment, but there are other causes, such as long-term stress and too-cool keeping conditions. Symptoms include labored breathing, wheezing, mucus build-up around the nostrils (do not confuse this with salt excretion; as previously noted, many species of lizards eliminate excess sodium from their bodies by sneezing it out, leaving some salt crystals around the nostrils), holding the head back and mouth agape for prolonged periods, and exuding mucus bubbles from the mouth and nose. If the latter two symptoms are present, your animal is in the later stages of a respiratory ailment and needs emergency vet care. Desert species are the most common victims of respiratory ailments.

If caught early enough, most respiratory ailments can be cured simply by increasing the heat in your animal's terrarium by a few degrees and, if the problem is humidity related, adjusting the humidity to the proper levels. If your lizard's condition does not improve in two or three days, seek veterinary attention.

Cryptosporidiosis

One dangerous internal parasite that cannot be eradicated in affected lizards is *Cryptosporidium*. The infection itself is called cryptosporidiosis, often shortened to "crypto" among herp hobbyists. Signs of crypto are similar to other parasitic infections and include vomiting, severe swelling and bloating, and rapid weight loss. Crypto is feared among hobbyists and commercial breeders because it can be present in an animal for two years or more before causing symptoms. Animals infected by crypto are doomed to die slowly and painfully and should be humanely euthanized by a veterinarian. Currently the incidence of crypto infection is increasing alarmingly in bearded dragons and leopard geckos.

Skin Diseases

Lesions, abscesses, blisters, and other nasty skin ailments can afflict your lizards. Typically, these ailments are brought about by damp, filthy living conditions. The affected areas may be discolored, they may run with pus, or there may be hard lumps or knots under the skin. Most often, skin problems show up on the bottom surfaces of your lizards: the feet, legs, belly, and lower portions of the tail.

As is true of most other ailments that afflict insect-eating lizards, this one's remedy begins by correcting the offending filthy or stressful living conditions; warm, dry (as appropriate for the species), hygienic conditions are in order. Treat the lesions themselves with a topical antibacterial wash followed by an application of antibiotic ointment. Keep a close eye on the sores. If they do not quickly improve, seek veterinary care.

Nodules or bumps under the skin are usually abscesses. These are encapsulated infections full of pus and pathogens. They could also be tumors, so this sign requires that you take your lizard to the vet. Your vet will test to see whether an abscess or a tumor is the problem. If it's an abscess, the veterinarian will lance, drain, and clean out the area; he is likely to prescribe antibiotics as well.

Metabolic Bone Disease

Metabolic bone disease ("MBD" to most herpers), is a degenerative condition that

This leopard gecko is emaciated due to a *Cryptosporidium* infestation. There is no cure for this dreaded parasite.

results from prolonged periods of inadequate nutrition or lack of proper lighting. Fast-growing hatchlings and juveniles are particularly at risk. Symptoms include: rubber-like flexibility of the limbs and lower jaw; deformities of the skull, spine, and tail; inability to feed; paralysis; and death.

MBD occurs when there is too little calcium or vitamin D in the lizard's diet. Vitamin D acts as a catalyst inside the lizard's body, and without it the lizard cannot absorb calcium. Secondary causes of MBD stem from inadequate lighting. Ultraviolet radiation (found in unfiltered natural sunlight) helps lizards to produce their own vitamin D and is beneficial for the metabolism as a whole. Curb MBD in your pets by supplementing their meals with calcium/vitamin D supplement once every two or three feedings and by offering your lizards ample exposure to either natural sunlight or special full-spectrum UV bulbs. For more details on proper lighting, see the housing chapter.

Injuries

Because of their small size and our propensity to handle them too frequently, insectivorous lizards can suffer from a wide range of physical injuries. These include fractured limbs (resulting from high falls), scratches or bites (from cage-mates or the family cat), burns, broken tails, etc. Minor cuts and abrasions may be cleansed with a povidone iodine or hydrogen peroxide solution and then treated with a topical antibiotic ointment. Deep wounds, cuts that refuse to close, puncture wounds, or other serious maladies will require a veterinarian's care. Broken limbs also require expert care. Burns are entirely preventable by providing proper heating apparatus and using a thermostat. All but the most minor burns

Dehydration

If your lizard's terrarium is too dry or you are not offering enough water in an acceptable form, your lizard will begin to dehydrate. There are many possible signs of dehydration: curled or withered scales, sunken eyes, loss of appetite, difficulty shedding, and constipation. Even low levels of dehydration damage the kidneys and lead to eventual kidney problems and a shortened lifespan. Jungle species commonly suffer from dehydration, and chameleons are especially prone to it.

The immediate solution is soaking your pet in a shallow dish of lukewarm water for half an hour. Long-term, solve this problem by raising the humidity in the terrarium and making sure your lizard has access to fresh water. Covering part of the top with cellophane and including live plants in the tank can help raise the humidity. A larger water dish (from which water vapor will evaporate into the tank) may also be in order.

Mouth Rot

Mouth rot, formally known as infectious stomatitis, is caused by any of several conditions but is most common when your reptile is kept at continually insufficient temperatures. Excessive exposure to cool conditions hinders the immune system, and an infection of the gums ensues. Poor nutrition can also be a factor.

You may first notice mouth rot by finding bacterial "cheese" developing inside the lizard's mouth. This causes discomfort, swelling, facial distortion, bleeding gums, lack of appetite, and finally tooth loss and death. In its early stages, mouth rot may be treated by gently prying open the lizard's mouth and swabbing away the lumps of yellowish exudate with a cotton swab soaked in povidone iodine or hydrogen peroxide. Raise the temperatures in the lizard's terrarium to appropriate levels. If the disease is more advanced, antibiotic treatment under a veterinarian's care should be administered.

require veterinary care. If your lizard suffers a very minor burn, bathe the wound in cool water and then treat it as you would a cut or abrasion.

Final Thoughts on Lizard Health Care

There are two factors that work against most common lizards in getting well once they've taken ill. First is the

Dehydration and low humidity can both cause shedding difficulties for lizards. A shedding collared lizard (*Crotaphytus collaris*) is shown here.

matter of size. The diminutive size of most of the lizards in this book makes them more susceptible to fatality once a disease takes hold, because the disease or ailment can more easily overwhelm a smaller body mass than a larger one. Most medicines used to treat herp-related ailments are measured for a more sizeable animal, such as a monitor or a python (and many medications are actually measured out for dogs, cats, or horses). Thus, this dosage must be *drastically* reduced when dealing with such small animals; an overdose of medicine can be just as fatal as the disease itself.

The second major factor working against the recovery of an insectivorous lizard is the cost of health care relative to the cost of the lizard. While it may seem absurd to spend 10 or 12 times the cost of the lizard on its health care, remember that taking on a pet is a moral responsibility that includes providing that pet with health care.

Remember that because we are dealing with such small animals, and because veterinarians' cures are costly and very difficult to administer to a lizard's tiny body, the best *cure* for insectivorous lizards is *prevention*. Follow the basic rules of feeding, husbandry, and handling, and you may never encounter one of the afflictions listed in this chapter. The long-term health of your animal is determined by the actions and decisions you make in daily care and maintenance.

Six Steps to Save Your Lizard

1. Identify the *exact* ailment as soon as possible. Take your animal to the vet if you are unsure.
2. Raise the temperature in the terrarium by 5 to 10°F (2.8 to 5.6°C). In the wild, lizards can often cure themselves by seeking out areas with a higher temperature and spending protracted periods basking. Continue to provide cooler retreats during this period.
3. Treat the ailment as best you can using commonly available remedies.
4. Reduce stress. Make the room surrounding the terrarium as stress-free as possible. Do not handle your lizard needlessly during this time period, and move the lizard to quarantine by itself.
5. If your lizard will eat, feed it as many gut-loaded feeders as it will take, as it will need all the nutrients it can get if it is to get well. Switching to a highly nutritious feeder, such as silkworms, is a good idea.
6. Once it is accurately diagnosed, treat the ailment accordingly.

Chapter 5

Species Profiles

This chapter is dedicated to giving you the lion's share of critical information you'll need to know before deciding upon and purchasing a particular species of lizard. It covers a large number of insectivorous lizard species. However, there are roughly 3,000 species of lizards, and most lizards are insect eaters. Clearly, this chapter cannot be comprehensive. Instead, it will introduce you to most of the lizards you are likely to see in pet stores and at herp expos.

Each lizard in this section has a profile detailing information important to the hobbyist. The profiles are categorized primarily by the biome type (desert, jungle, woodland, savanna, montane, etc.) in which the species are found. They are further broken down by terms of names (common and scientific), housing requirements, average adult size, and overall pet suitability, followed by more detailed comments about the lizard. Pet suitability is ranked on a scale from 1 to 5, with 5 being a difficult-to-keep species that should not be purchased by beginning hobbyists, 4 is slightly easier to maintain, 3 is the average specimen with which a dedicated beginner can experience success, 2 is a fine, hardy animal, and any lizard that is classified as a 1 is a superior choice for both beginners and experienced keepers alike. In some cases, an otherwise durable and hardy species may be given a higher number based on an aggressive disposition or a very shy, retiring nature (a species that goes to great lengths to stay totally hidden seldom makes for a rewarding captive for the beginning hobbyist).

While there are far too many insectivorous lizard species in existence to describe here, I have highlighted some of the most popularly kept species, as well as some old-time favorites that still appear occasionally in the pet field. Bear in mind also that some of the most popular species in the herp hobby today (leopard geckos, for example) get some coverage here, but since there are already so many solid books on the care and maintenance of these delightful lizards, I will not spend too much time discussing them. Because so many species may have the same basic requirements as other members of the same genus or family, in some places only one species in the group is covered. For example, there are several varieties of *Phrynosoma* (horned lizards), but the captive requirements of these animals are so similar that mentioning all of the species individually would quickly become redundant.

The bearded dragon is one of the most highly recommended lizards for hobbyists; it is both hardy and normally quite docile.

Desert Species

Desert species often have high metabolic rates, and the diurnal species require higher temperatures than the lizards from any other biome type. Conversely, these lizards also require dense patches of shade and cooling shadow in which they may escape the blazing heat of the desert sun. Many desert lizards need a nighttime temperature that is much lower than the daytime temperature; most deserts are quite cool—even cold—at night.

Bearded Dragon (*Pogona vitticeps*)

Range: Extensive throughout Australia.

Size: May attain 21-22 inches (53.3-56 cm)

Diet: Insects, vegetables, mice. For adults, the diet should be roughly 50 percent insects and 50 percent greens and other vegetables.

Longevity: May exceed ten years with excellent care.

Terrarium Size: Surface area is more important than height, although bearded dragons will climb if given the opportunity. A 15-gallon (56.8-l) tank will support a juvenile, while a 55-gallon (208.2-l) can serve as home to an adult. Territorial by nature, bearded dragons always fare better the more space they have in which to roam.

Temperatures: Ambient in mid 80s (about 28°C) with hot spot reaching 105°F (40.6°C).

Lighting: 10 to 12 hours daily; high UVB levels required.

Description: Truly dragon-like in appearance, these lizards wear a basal coloration that matches the tawny, gravel-strewn soils of the Australian deserts: tan and yellowish on a reddish to dun or brown backdrop. Small conical and rugged scales adorn the dorsum and flanks, while the belly is smooth and soft. Taking its common name from the "beard" of conical scales that it may flare while defending its territory or when confronting a would-be predator, this lizard's throat area can expand and bristle during times of stress; males' beards may change from blackish to dark bluish during the mating season or when displaying.

Beginner's Top Ten

The following list contains some of the hardiest and easiest lizard species to maintain in the captive environment. Any newcomer to the herp hobby is advised to stick to these ten species when choosing his or her first insectivorous lizard.

- African fat-tailed gecko
- Anole (green or brown)
- Armadillo lizard
- Bearded dragon
- Curly-tailed lizard
- Leopard gecko
- Moorish gecko
- Ocellated skink
- Schneider's skink
- Sudan plated lizard

Pet Suitability: 1. Bearded dragons are hardy, intelligent, attractive, and easily maintained.

Collared Lizard (*Crotaphytus collaris*)

Range: Extensive through the American Southwest.

Size: 8-14 inches (20.3-35.6 cm); males are by far the larger of the two sexes.

Diet: Anything that moves. Captive diet for adults should be composed of roughly 70 percent gut-loaded insects and 30 percent vertebrate protein (e.g., pinkie mice, smaller lizards). Collared lizards recently collected from the wild may not drink water from a dish; sprinkle water droplets on a stone early in the morning for the lizard to lap up until it becomes acclimated to drinking standing water from a dish.

Longevity: Recorded longevity exceeds ten years.

Terrarium Size: Large. Collared lizards need wide, open spaces in which to roam. A single specimen will do well in a 55-gallon (208.2-l) or larger environment. They are fond of perching on tall rocks, so providing some climbing material is good idea.

Temperatures: Fond of basking, this reptile requires an ambient range of 83-86° (28.3-30°C) with a hot spot of up to 115° F (46.1°C). Nightly drops may fall into the 60s (as low as 17°C) with no ill effects.

Lighting: Bright throughout the day, with high levels of UVB.

Although they are beautiful and interesting, collared lizards can be very aggressive.

Description: Collared lizards take their common name from the black band that runs almost entirely around their necks (at least in males; a female's collar may be broken or indistinct). These are large, powerfully built lizards with an attitude to match. Capable of fleeing predators or running down prey on only their hind legs, these stocky reptiles have a definite dinosaur-like appearance to them.

When cornered or threatened, collared lizards will not hesitate to defend themselves violently. Typical defense behavior includes the lizard's rearing on its hind legs and leaping toward the face of its attacker, biting *hard,* and hanging on. It's no rare thing for an unwary attacker to leave a confrontation with a collared lizard bloodied and scarred. Collared lizards are one of the most beautiful species found in North America. Particularly vibrant during mating season, males will sport emerald green hues along their flanks and throat, with ruddy orange splashes over the head and forequarters. The dorsum is heavily speckled in whitish and yellow spots. When gravid, female collared lizards display reddish orange spots on their forequarters.

There are several other species and subspecies of collared lizards. The care for them is identical. For the hobbyist's purposes, they differ mostly in color and price.

Pet Suitability: 3. Collared lizards are not for everyone, and I do not recommend them as a lizard for the newcomer to the hobby. Couple their need for large spaces with their sometimes feisty disposition and it's easy to see why these reptiles are best left to more experienced folks. Bear in mind that these lizards are devout carnivores that will kill and eat any other lizard with which they are housed, including other members of their own species!

Five More Desert Lizards

Here are five more lizard species that will thrive in a desert terrarium. Be sure to research the exact needs of any species you plan to keep.

clown agama (*Laudakia stellio*)
fringe-toed lizards (*Uma* spp.)
ground gecko (*Chondrodactylus angulifer*)
Lawson's dragon (*Pogona henrylawsoni*)
web-footed gecko (*Palmatogecko* spp.)

Common Tree Lizard (*Urosaurus ornatus*)

Range: Texas west to southern California and northern Mexico; north through Utah.

Size: 4-6.5 inches (10.2-16.5 cm)

Diet: Fond of adult *Tenebrio* beetles and small crickets, tree lizards will also accept wax worms, mealworms, etc.

Longevity: May exceed four years.

Terrarium Size: Despite their being desert animals, tree lizards are arboreal and must have plenty of vertical climbing space in the form of rocks, dry limbs, etc. A tall tank is more important than a broad one in this case. Both natural (cork bark, sand-blasted grape vine, driftwood, etc.) and artificial climbing structures will suffice. The tank should be 10 gallons (37.9 l) for single specimens; larger for communities.

Temperatures: 82-84° F (27.8-29°C) ambient with a basking spot in the mid-90s (34-36°C). Nightly drop of about 10°F (5.5°C) is fine.

Lighting: UV lighting should be available for several hours daily, but these lizards do not need it all day. In the wild, tree lizards seek rocky crevices or cedar canopies in order to escape the blazing desert sun during the heat of the day. They will again bask in the late afternoon hours.

Despite being sold as food for snakes, common tree lizards make good pets and adapt well to terrarium life.

Description: Common tree lizards are slim, agile predators whose fleetness of foot and adept climbing skills keep them in pursuit of prey and out of the jaws of predators. Wearing a base coat of gray to sandy-tan with dorsal chevrons of black to charcoal, the common tree lizard sports its most vibrant coloration in its tail. Broad at the base and rapidly tapering into a whip-like shape, the tail of the tree lizard may be yellow to orange or even reddish in some specimens. Warm, stress-free animals are more brightly colored than are cool, ill, or highly stressed individuals.

Active primarily during the early morning hours, these lizards seek shelter from the sweltering desert sun by climbing into cedar trees or into the crevices of fence posts or dead standing timber. Activity again rises during the late afternoon and early evening hours.

Pet Suitability: 2. Frequently encountered in the pet trade as "feeders" for lizard-eating snakes, common tree lizards make excellent captives. They tend to be wary and may hide amidst rock cover frequently. Other *Urosaurus* species encountered in the pet trade (canyon tree lizard, eastern tree lizard, and small-scaled tree lizard) may be housed under similar conditions.

Curly-Tailed Lizard (*Leiocephalus* spp.)

Range: Extensive throughout the Caribbean, including the Bahamas, and introduced to southern Florida via terrarium escapees and discarded pets.

Size: 7 to 10.5 inches (17.8-26.7 cm)

Diet: Insects of all kinds.

Longevity: Unknown, though some reports of seven-year-old specimens are within reason.

Terrarium Size: Curly-tailed lizards (usually called curly-tails) are primarily terrestrial animals that need plenty of horizontal space. A tank with a large floor space therefore is in order. A single specimen may thrive in a 20-gallon (75.7-l) enclosure, while a colony will require a 40- to 55-gallon (151.4-208.2-l) habitat.

Temperatures: Fond of early morning and late afternoon basking, these hardy reptiles enjoy ambient temperatures in the low to mid 80s (27.2-29.4°C) with a basking spot of roughly 95°-100° F (35-37.8°C). As with all other captive lizards, they should be supplied with adequate cooler retreats for thermoregulation.

Lighting: 8 to 12 hours of full-spectrum ultraviolet light.

Description: Because so many species and subspecies of curly-tailed lizard exist throughout the tropics of the Caribbean and surrounding islands (as well as the continental United States), it is very likely impossible to know exactly which one you have. Most of the ones in the hobby are from Florida and Haiti, but some are imported from other islands.

Taking its common name from its ridged tail, which it curls, twitches, and flicks in order to communicate with others of its own kind, this lizard also employs its tail as a unique defensive tool. It is no secret that many lizard species will drop their tails when accosted by a predator and that the flicking, twitching tail will act as a decoy while the lizard beats a hasty retreat. But the curly-tailed lizard takes this survival strategy one step further. When approached by a predator, the lizard will hold its head, body, and legs perfectly still while whipping its tail wildly and erratically about. This flailing tail functions as a lure to attract the

A number of curly-tailed lizard species originate in Haiti. Two of the most common ones in the hobby are *L. schreibersi* (below) and *L. personatus* (above).

predator's attention. When the strike comes, it is almost always directed toward the active tail and not at the lizard itself. Thus the curly-tail lives to fight another day.

These lizards seldom venture into tall trees or any other perch that is more than a few feet off the ground. As a result of their devoutly ground-going lifestyle, these lizards are commonly preyed upon by snakes; ironically, the snakes are seldom fooled by the whiplash behavior of the lizard's tail. Curly-tails shelter in burrows they dig themselves. Provide your curly-tails with a sandy substrate so they can perform this behavior. As a general rule, curly-tailed lizards will thrive in either a desert or savanna habitat, so long as they are maintained at a relative humidity lower than 65 percent. Construct a hide with moist damp substrate into which the lizard may retreat, but also keep drier places in the tank for basking as well. **Pet Suitability:** 1. An underrated lizard, the curly-tailed lizard is among the most hardy, active, and handle-friendly small lizards that a hobbyist could ever hope for. A best-bet all around.

Side-Blotched Lizard (*Uta stansburiana*)

Range: New Mexico, Texas, northern Mexico.
Size: To 6 inches (15.2 cm)
Diet: Insects and other invertebrates.
Longevity: May exceed five years.
Terrarium Size: Side-blotched lizards are active animals, and a long and wide terrarium is a must. Despite their small size, I recommend nothing shy of a 30-gallon (113.5-l) tank outfitted with ample vertical climbing structures.

Temperatures: Maintain ambient temperatures of 80°-86° F (26.7-30°C) with a basking area of 95°F (35°C). Nightly drops of up to 10° (5.6°C) are sufficient.
Lighting: Eight to ten hours of full-spectrum UVB
Description: Native to the scrub and deserts of the American Southwest, these lizards are one of the most commonly encountered species within their range.

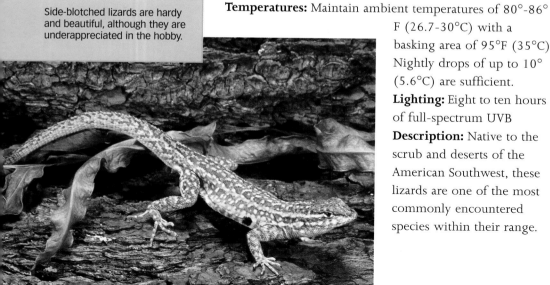

Side-blotched lizards are hardy and beautiful, although they are underappreciated in the hobby.

Fond of basking on fence posts or on the sides of small trees, they actively hunt prey during all daylight hours.

Sporting a base coloration of brown to sandy gray, these lizards take their common name from the blue-black blotch that occurs on their lateral flanks, just behind either forelimb. Males may also display radiant blue to greenish speckling along their tails and dorsum; this color typically fades when the lizard is frightened or stressed.

Pet Suitability: 1. Side-blotched lizards are one of my personal favorites in that they are so colorful and active. It's no rare thing for a side-blotched lizard to approach the glass of the tank when its keeper enters the room. It may almost beg like a dog to be fed, and keepers often enjoy feeding their scaly pets mealworms or crickets from their fingertips. Hardy, docile, and beautiful, this species is an underappreciated but excellent pet.

Earless Lizard (*Holbrookia spp.*)

Range: Extensive throughout the American West.

Size: To just under 6 inches (15.2 cm) depending on the subspecies in question.

Diet: Insects and other invertebrates.

Longevity: Unknown, though four years or more is a reasonable assumption based on current data.

Terrarium Size: Earless lizards are ground-going runners, and as such they require spacious environs. A tank that stresses surface area over vertical height is definitely advisable. I recommend nothing less than a 55-gallon terrarium (208.2-l) for one to three individuals.

Temperatures: Earless lizards like it hot; ambient temps in the mid-80s (about 28-30°C) with a basking spot (or two) in the 100-110° (37.8-43.3°C) range are preferable. Cooler retreats and a nighttime temperature drop are also mandatory.

Lighting: 12-14 hours of UVB exposure.

Description: Wiry, fast, and extremely wary reptiles, the earless lizards are mottled in earth-tone hues of gray, tan, and sandy yellow. Basking for hours in the early morning sun, these lizards sit on open sand or atop low rocky outcroppings with their heads held high and their eyes open for danger, so they are a very difficult species for any predator to approach.

Seldom climbing any higher than a few feet (a

Female side-blotched lizards are less colorful than the males, and their blotch is much less distinct.

meter or so) off the ground, these terrestrial lizards instead seek cover under rocks or even under the sand; if there is no other escape, an earless lizard will not hesitate to "dive" under the surface of loose sand to escape danger. Taking their common name from the fact that they lack an exterior ear opening (though they are not truly deaf), these swift hunters spend their days in search of spiders, beetles, and careless flies and cicadas. Splayed legs and broad feet help these animals gain superior footing atop loose sand.

Pet Suitability: 3. If you can offer these lizards enough room to roam, a small colony of earless lizards can make a unique addition to any herp collection. Hobbyists wishing to own pet-type lizards should look elsewhere, as the wary earless lizards will not tolerate handling.

Frog-Eyed Gecko (*Teratoscincus scincus*)

Range: Southern Asia to Arabian Peninsula

Size: To 7 inches (17.8 cm).

Diet: Insects. Gut-loading of crickets is highly recommended; gravid females in particular need additional calcium added to each meal.

Communal Living

Sometimes hobbyists get infatuated with the idea of housing several lizards in the same terrarium. While this idea is not completely impossible, there are some considerations to take into account before jumping headlong into this project.

First, you must make sure that the lizard species you choose to mix will cohabit peacefully. Many lizards, such as chameleons and terrestrial geckos, may nip or bite smaller lizards out of territoriality, aggression, or predation. Successful cohabitation also requires that all the lizards have similar requirements. Housing a desert lizard and a rainforest lizard together will not work.

Another thing to consider is that multiple males of the same species may become extraordinarily territorial with one another and may even fight to the death. A final consideration is the welfare of any female lizards in the tank. Male lizards of many species can get quite frisky, and a lone female in the tank will soon be "mated to death" by the throng of amorous males. So do some homework on the exact species you wish to keep together, and make sure each lizard with thrive together.

Longevity: Eight or more years.

Terrarium: As a terrestrial roamer, the frog-eyed gecko needs a long, wide tank, but not an especially tall one. Most experts agree that a 30-inch long x 12-inch wide (76.2 x 30.5 cm) tank is sufficient for up to three individuals.

The earless lizards living in white sand deserts have developed a matching pale coloration to provide camouflage.

Lighting: Frog-eyed geckos will benefit from full-spectrum lighting, provided they expose themselves to it. These animals are powerfully nocturnal, however, and basking is a rarity.

Temperature: 85° (29.4°C) with hot spot of about 100° (37.7°C). Cool retreats and a nighttime temperature drop are critical to the health of this species.

Description: Frog-eyed geckos (also called wonder geckos and fish-scaled geckos) are terrestrial and exceedingly fond of burrowing. Hiding by day in their stable moist and deep burrows, these demure lizards emerge at dusk for a night of foraging for beetles, scorpions, and locusts.

The scales along the body of the frog-eyed gecko are large and layered like shingles; they are much like the scales of a fish. These scales (and the underlying skin) are *very* fragile, however, and can easily be rubbed off if the lizard is grabbed or picked up suddenly. Despite their thriving in desert environments, these geckos are deeply dependent on moisture, which enters and exits their skin during respiration. If kept in a dry terrarium without a deep, moist burrow in which to retreat, a frog-eyed gecko will soon perish. This is one desert lizard that should have access to a small water bowl at all times.

Several species of frog-eyed geckos are available in the hobby, with at least three being captive bred. This is *T. scincus*, the common frog-eyed gecko.

Breeding females can produce nearly three dozen eggs in a single season, which will readily deplete her calcium stores. Gravid females *absolutely must* be supplied with additional calcium and mineral supplements.

There are several species of *Teratoscincus* available in the pet trade. The care for the different species is very similar, although some prefer cooler temperatures. Captive-bred individuals are available through online vendors and at larger herp expos.

Pet Suitability: 5. I cannot stress enough the necessity for years of experience in dealing with desert-dwelling geckos on the part of the keeper; these fragile animals are best left to the experts.

Granite Spiny Lizard (*Sceloporus orcutti*)

Range: Extreme southern California, Baja Peninsula.

Size: Adults may range from 8-10.5 inches (20.3-26.7 cm).

Diet: All insects are readily accepted, and dandelions and other flowers are also taken on occasion.

Longevity: Sadly, captive longevity is poorly known, as these animals typically do not receive adequate care in the terrarium. Wild specimens may live for several years.

Terrarium Size: One adult granite spiny lizard may fare well in a 30-gallon (113.5-l) tank, provided that it has ample rockwork for climbing and hiding. Excellent ventilation and low relative humidity are mandatory for the long-term survival of this species. No species of

Sceloporus will thrive in a Spartan or non-naturalistic terrarium.

Temperatures: Hot! Granite spiny lizards need ambient daytime temperatures around 85°F (29.4°C) with hot spots of 100°-110° (37.8-43.3°C) and cooler retreats.

Lighting: Bright, high-intensity, full-spectrum lighting that provides high levels of UVB.

Description: Perhaps the most visually stunning lizard on the North American continent, the granite spiny lizard wears a virtual rainbow of colors: burnished copper to black with flecks and speckles of turquoise to metallic lavender on each scale. Aquamarine bands may encircle the tail and limbs of particularly striking specimens. Males are distinctly more vivid than females, though the females still bear stunning coloration. The head is large, with powerful jaws. The body is of stocky build, denoting a swift runner and skilled climber.

Complete insectivores, granite spiny lizards attack and devour their invertebrate prey with surprising speed and ferocity. Keen eyesight keeps granite spiny lizards on the alert, and they will quickly flee into a rocky crevice when danger draws near. Although they are overall hardy, these lizards are prone to blisters when kept in overly damp conditions.

A wide variety of *Sceloporus* lizards occur in the pet trade, so it is always important to make certain of what species you are purchasing, as different species may have different captive care requirements depending on what part of the nation or world they come from. Most fare well in desert or savanna setups, but their needs vary greatly.

Pet Suitability: 3. Because of their stunning coloration, these animals are frequently purchased suddenly and without the hobbyist's having ample information on the animal's long-term care requirements. These hardy, active lizards are demanding in terms of heat and lighting, but the aesthetic rewards of successfully keeping one are great. Provided with ample heat, aridity, and appropriate foods, this species can make an excellent captive for the experienced and dedicated lizard enthusiast.

Granite spiny lizards and most other swifts require hot and dry conditions and a sizable terrarium.

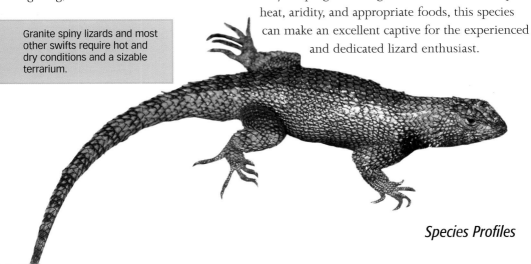

Leopard Gecko (*Eublepharis macularius*)

Range: Pakistan, Turkmenistan, and northwestern India.

Size: Up to 8 inches (20.3 cm)

Diet: Insects.

Longevity: May exceed 20 years.

Terrarium Size: Leopard geckos are slow-moving terrestrial reptiles that need minimal space to roam. An adult leopard gecko can be sufficiently housed in a 15-gallon (56.8-l) terrarium. Tank height is of negligible importance. Having a humidified hiding area is highly recommended.

Temperatures: Provide a thermal gradient ranging from 75°F (23.9°C) at one side of the cage to the upper 80s (30.5-31°C) at the other. Because of their nocturnal lifestyle, leopard geckos and their relatives seldom bask for long periods of time.

Lighting: 10-14 hours per day; photoperiod is particularly important if you are planning a breeding project with your geckos. Ultraviolet light is not necessary (as these reptiles often avoid exposure to intense lights), but is advisable.

Description: Terrestrial, thick bodied, and slow moving, the species of the family Eublepharidae are the only geckos with moveable eyelids. This family includes the leopard geckos (*Eublepharis*), fat-tailed geckos (*Hemitheconyx*), banded geckos (*Coleonyx*), cat geckos (*Aeluroscalabotes*), cave geckos (*Goniurosaurus*), and gully geckos (*Holodactylus*). Of these, only the first three are suitable for most hobbyists. The others are rather rare and specialized. All species are almost exclusively nocturnal.

The desert spiny lizard (*S. magister magister*) ranges over a large area of the western U.S. It can be kept much like a granite spiny lizard.

Fond of hiding amidst rocky outcroppings, leopard geckos exhibit a curiously feline-like behavior when stalking prey. As the lizard zeroes-in for the kill, it waggles its tail back and forth in rapid, cat-like fashion just before striking. Coloration is highly variable. Leopard geckos wear a base color of yellow with purple to brownish maroon splotches and spots, but they have been bred in a number of color morphs, including albino, snow, patternless, and striped. Leopard geckos and most other eublepharids do well in small colonies, as long as only one male is present.

Pet Suitability: 1. The leopard gecko is my absolute top recommendation to any hobbyist of any experience level. These lizards are gentle, cute (they seem to be wearing a perpetual dreamy-eyed smile), and hardy, and they seem to enjoy being taken out and held, especially when they are mature (neonates and juveniles may be a bit skittish). The banded geckos of North and Central America also make excellent and long-lived pets, although because of their smaller size and intolerance of handling, they rank a 2. While the captive conditions described here are suitable for most eublepharids, you should do plenty of extra research on the exact species you are interested in before making your purchase.

Most adult leopard geckos are docile and tolerant of handling.

Leopard Lizard (*Gambelia wislizenii*)

Range: Southern Idaho south through northern Mexico, east to extreme western Texas.

Size: To 15.5 inches (39.4 cm)

Diet: Insects, pinkie mice, small lizards. May be maintained on a captive diet of 80 percent gut-loaded insects and 20 percent vertebrate protein in the form of pinkie mice.

Longevity: Comparable to the collared lizard; ten years or so

Terrarium Size: 50 gallons (189.3 l) is suitable for one, as this active predator needs plenty of room to roam.

Temperatures: Ambient of 84-88°F (28.9-31.1°C) with hot spots reaching 110° F (43.3°C). Cool retreats (rocky crevices, PVC pipe burrows, etc.) are mandatory for thermoregulation; a nighttime drop of at least 10°F (5.6°C) is recommended.

Lighting: 10-12 hours of full-spectrum, high-intensity UVB.

Description: Cannibalistic and voracious predators, leopard lizards are the fiercest lizard hunters throughout their range. Wearing a sandy-tan base color dappled with reddish dots and cream-colored bands across the dorsum, this lizard is supremely camouflaged in the rocky rubble and scrubby grass of its western environment. Such camouflage aids it in stalking prey and avoiding predation. The arrow-shaped snout and heavily scaled head suggest this lizard's propensity for rooting buried or hiding prey items out of their rocky or wooden retreats. Very fleet of foot, the leopard lizard is no less skilled at running down and subduing prey as it is at ambushing it. As might be expected, the leopard lizard is also quite skittish and will flee danger when possible. However, it will not hesitate to defend itself violently when cornered. This lizard can inflict a painful, bloody bite. Never house this lizard with lizards of another species.

Pet Suitability: 4. The leopard lizard (all subspecies included) is declining in the wild as the result of habitat loss, so it is now listed by the federal government as endangered. *Never* purchase wild-caught individuals, as they may have been illegally poached from nature. Captive-breeding projects do, however, supply the occasional leopard lizard to the pet trade legally. Because of this lizard's need for space and its semi-aggressive behaviors, I cannot recommend it to most hobbyists. If you are skilled in dealing with desert lizards, however, a leopard lizard can present a unique and rewarding challenge.

Ocellated Skink (*Chalcides ocellatus*)

Range: Mediterranean region; Italy, Greece, and North Africa to northwestern India.

Size: Highly variable; may range from only 6 inches to over 12 inches (15.2-30.5 cm).

Diet: Invertebrates.

Longevity: Eight years or more is not uncommon.

Terrarium Size: Variable depending on the size of your pet; larger animals require larger quarters, with a 15-gallon (56.8-l) tank being suitable for a small individual. Sandy substrate should measure no less than

Western banded geckos (*Coleonyx variegatus*) can be kept much like leopard geckos, although they are smaller and should not be handled.

5 inches (12.7 cm) deep. Supply this skink with plenty of hideaways, though it is an accomplished sand swimmer in its own right.

Temperatures: Provide a hot spot of 105° F (40.6) with ambient temperature of not less than 82°F (27.8°C). A large temperature drop at night is a good idea.

Lighting: 10-12 hours of full-spectrum lighting.

Description: A very sleek-scaled lizard, the torpedo-shaped ocellated skink has reduced legs and small eyes; both adaptations indicative of a subterranean lifestyle. While it does enjoy basking, this skink is indeed fond of slinking through loose sand and surface debris in search of spiders, grubs, and other invertebrates.

Taking its common name from the broken columns of white-centered spots (or ocelli) lining its dorsum, this skink also wears light blue spots along the lower jaw and neck region. Surprisingly fast-moving and agile, the ocellated skink will not hesitate to seek cover under nearby rocks or dead timber should a predator draw near.

Pet Suitability: 1. Popular among European hobbyists, the ocellated skink is only recently coming into its own in the United States. Durable and quietly attractive, these demure reptiles are very hardy. Be sure to offer this species additional moisture via a PVC pipe as described for the sandfish skink.

Sandfish Skink (*Scincus scincus*)

Range: Northern Africa to the Middle East

Size: 4 to 6 inches (10.2-15.2 cm) or slightly longer depending on subspecies; males larger than females.

Diet: Wax worms and mealworms are favorites of the sandfish, as are adult *Tenebrio* beetles; other invertebrates are accepted.

Ocellated skinks require a deep sandy substrate in which they can burrow.

Longevity: May exceed ten years in captivity; shorter in the wild.

Terrarium Size: 30-gallon (113.6-l) "long" tank minimum. These burrowing lizards need a lot of floor space and deep sandy substrate.

Lighting: Eight to ten hours of full-spectrum light so long as the animal basks; if after some months of keeping, you know your lizard basks only at certain times of the day, burn your UV bulbs only during those times, as it is wasteful and useless to illuminate empty sand. The time spent basking will largely vary based on individual skinks.

Temperatures: Daily ambient temperatures not to exceed 85° F (29.4°C), with a basking spot of 100-110° F (37.8-43.3°C). Nightly drop of around 10°F (5.6°C) preferred.

Description: One of the most unique insectivorous lizard species in the industry today, the sandfish skink (roughly ten subspecies of which occur in the US pet trade) has a flattened wedge-shaped head with a close-sealing countersunk mouth, a compressed sleek body, smooth scales, and flanged toes on its feet. All of these specialized adaptations function to help this lizard to literally swim through the loose sands of its desert homeland at amazing speeds.

Sandfish possess dorsal bands of yellowish to ochre across an alabaster to silvery base. These skinks hunt grubs, larvae, and small beetles by feeling the vibrations of the wriggling insect through the sand and emerging underneath the insect to make a surprise attack from below. It is this same sensitivity to vibrations in the sand that alerts these skinks when predators are near.

Water sandfish skinks by placing an upright length of PVC piping in one corner of the tank with the end nestled close to the bottom glass of the tank. Pour small amounts of water down this pipe every 10-14 days. Sandfish will obtain virtually all necessary moisture through this slightly moist layer of sand deep in the tank, as well as from the bodies of their prey.

Pet Suitability: 1. The sandfish skink is docile, attractive, low maintenance, and very hardy. Given ample temperatures and deep sand (at least 7 inches (17.8 cm) in depth) in which to navigate, these animals can bring their keeper years of enjoyment.

Sudan Plated Lizard *(Gerrhosaurus major)*

Range: Eastern Africa. Most specimens come from Sudan and Mozambique.

Size: Very large; adults may exceed 19 inches (48.3 cm) in length.

The sandfish earned its name from its ability to seemingly swim through the sand without effort.

Diet: All manner of insects and some vegetation (green beans, grapes, melons, and dandelion heads are taken with relish). Captive specimens may also take pinkie mice and canned reptile foods as well as canned cat/dog foods. Sweet fruits, such as kiwi, are also occasionally taken. This lizard appreciates a light daily misting.

Longevity: With proper care, ten years or more is common.

Terrarium Size: As large as possible. Custom-made enclosures are a good idea, as you may construct them specifically to meet the surface-area needs of this large lizard.

Temperatures: Daily ambient temperatures of 80°-82° F(26.7-27.8°C) with a basking spot of 94-96°F (34.4-35.6°C) are suitable, as are nightly drops of 10°-15° F (5.6-8.3°C).

Lighting: 12-14 hours of full-spectrum lighting.

Description: Wearing a dark brown coat of heavy plates, the Sudan plated lizard has a blocky build with a powerful tail and a wedge-shaped head. The body is divided laterally with a flap of skin between the upper and lower "halves" to allow the animal to swallow large meals. The legs are surprisingly strong, as are the jaws, making this terrestrial lizard an accomplished predator and burrower. It also is capable of both ambush hunting as well as running down fleeing prey items. In the wild, a male will often establish a home territory and hoard a harem of females, which he will defend against both predators and rival males alike.

Pet Suitability: 1. It is with great pleasure that I recommend the Sudan plated lizard to any and all hobbyists. This is a rough-and-tumble, non-aggressive, hardy, and loveable captive. This lizard seems to enjoy being taken out of its terrarium and handled regularly. However, caution must be exercised during feeding time, as this lizard may not always know where the prey item stops and its keeper's fingers begin! The powerful jaws of an otherwise benign and well-meaning Sudan plated lizard can accidentally inflict a painful and bloody bite.

Sudan plated lizards are hardy and docile, but unfortunately they are rarely captive bred.

Be aware also that newly imported specimens often carry a heavy internal parasite load. Once cleansed of its parasites and healthy, this stalwart reptile can easily bring a decade of reptilian joy to its keeper. More keepers should work with trying to breed this exceptional pet lizard.

Sungazer (*Cordylus giganteus*)

Range: Southern portion of Africa.

Size: 8-15.5 inches (20.3-39.3 cm).

Diet: Insects. Captive diet should be as varied as possible.

Longevity: Ten years or more if housed properly.

Terrarium Size: As large as possible with deep (length of the lizard) sand and peat substrate and rocky hiding and climbing areas (crags, caves, cliffs, etc.); a 55-gallon (208.-l) tank is the minimum acceptable size, though a 75-gallon (284-l) or larger setup is preferred.

Temperatures: Daily ambient of low to mid 80s (26.7-30°C) with one or more basking hot spots of 100° Fahrenheit.

Lighting: No less than 14 hours per day of full-spectrum lighting.

Description: The sungazer, one of the family of "girdle-tailed" lizards, is one of the most unforgettable lizards anyone could ever encounter. With its spiky, plate mail-like scales, heavily armored tail, and flanged, triangular skull, this reptile resembles a holdover from the days of the dinosaurs. Taking its common name from its unusually devout basking behaviors, the sungazer will spend hours each morning sitting motionless in the sun, with its body turned broad-side to the rays and its head held aloft and pointed directly at the sun. After reaching its optimum temperature, the sungazer will scuttle off to hunt spiders, grasshoppers,

Sungazers bask for long periods of time, often facing the sun directly, which is how they acquired their common name.

Along with being very difficult to keep, the Texas horned lizard is protected by law, and hobbyists should not purchase or collect it.

and other invertebrate prey.

These lizards are communal and may live in large numbers inside deep burrows (each animal living in its own burrow amid a network of burrows constructed closely together) under stones or near other protective structure. If molested, the sungazer will flee into its burrow, lash its tail at its attacker, and anchor the backwards-pointing spines on its skull into the roof of the burrow should the predator try to pull it out of its lair.

Pet Suitability: 3. These animals simply must have a dedicated keeper who is willing to give them the time, money (full-spectrum bulbs and the electricity to run them can get expensive), and effort they need. Usually commanding a high price in pet stores and through specialized dealers, the sungazer is definitely not a buy-on-a-whim kind of lizard.

Texas Horned Lizard *(Phrynosoma cornutum)*

Range: Kansas to Texas and west to Arizona. Also found in Louisiana and introduced into northern Florida. This species is protected by law in much of its naturally occurring range.

Size: Large adults may exceed 7 inches (17.8 cm) long; the head and body make up most of this length.

Diet: Highly specialized. Texas horned lizards must be supplied with some variety of ant as at least 30 percent of its staple diet for long-term survival. Crickets,

Smaller Plates

Two smaller species of *Gerrhosaurus*, the yellow-throated plated lizard (*G. flavigularis*) and the black-lined plated lizard (*G. nigrolineatus*) are slightly smaller and appear in the US pet trade occasionally. Care for these subspecies is as described for *G. major*.

The round-tailed horned lizard ranges from central Texas to western Arizona and south into Mexico.

mealworms, and wax worms may compose the remaining diet. Dust every third meal.

Longevity: Under ideal conditions (lots of ants), the lifespan of a Texas horned lizard may exceed five to eight years in captivity. Most specimens, however, die of malnourishment in less than a year after purchase.

Terrarium Size: Not a wide-roaming species, the Texas horned lizard may fare well in a 20-gallon (75.7-l) tank that supplies both ample floor space and extensive rockwork for climbing, basking, and hiding.

Temperatures: Lovers of heat, these lizards do best with an ambient temperature of 80°F (26.7°C) and a basking spot of 100-110° F (37.8-43.3°C). Nightly drops of no more than 15°F (8.3°C) suffice.

Lighting: 12-14 hours of full-spectrum lighting.

Description: The classic American "horned toads" that so many of us had as kids, these animals are truly an oddball species among lizards. With a round, broad head that is crested in a row of bony spurs and spikes extending backward from the base of the skull and the ability to squirt blood at attackers from the corners of their eyes when agitated, the Texas horned lizards have a definite prehistoric air about them, which explains the popularity they've enjoyed over the years. Though gentle handling may not be out of the question, recently captured horned lizards may puff up their bodies, hiss aggressively, or even inflict a painful little bite if agitated enough.

Avoid the Horns

Several other horned lizards occur in the pet trade; the most commonly encountered of these is the round-tailed horned lizard (*P. modestum*). The desert horned lizard (*P. platyrhinos*) also is available on occasion. Like the Texas species, the other horned lizards are difficult to keep, requiring a diet mostly of ants. Even experienced hobbyists should think twice before purchasing a horned lizard.

Pet Suitability: 5. Despite my personal love for these rugged little guys, I have to rank the Texas horned lizards as an animal for experienced hobbyists only. As long as the hobbyist has a continual supply of small ants to feed their lizard, a horned lizard may thrive for some years. However, this endless supply of tiny invertebrates is not an easy order to fill. In virtually all cases, the captive horned lizard will suffer and die from poor nutrition within a year. Heat and ants are crucial to a successful endeavor. Additionally, Texas horned lizards are widely protected by law, and only captive-bred animals should be purchased. Under no circumstance whatsoever should a Texas horned lizard be captured from the wild. Other horned lizard species are just as difficult to keep.

Whiptail Lizards (*Cnemidophorus* spp.)

Range: Discontinuous throughout the United States to South America.

Size: To 18 inches (45.7 cm); most whiptails are smaller, however. Claims of much larger (30 inches [76.2 cm]) whiptails also exist.

Diet: Insects. Larger whiptails will accept small rodents, while some species will also accept fruits, fresh flowers, and buds.

Longevity: Highly variable between species, though common life span typically exceeds five years for small specimens and may exceed ten years for larger, more robust species.

Terrarium Size: There are a great many variables within the whiptail terrarium depending on which species you wish to keep and what habitat they hail from (jungle or desert, for example). For all these variations, however, there is one definite constant in the whiptail terrarium: lots of horizontal space. These lizards require very large environs, as they run and dart over a much broader range than most other pet lizards. Always keep your whiptails in as large a tank as you possibly can.

The western whiptail (*C. tigris*) has a number of subspecies and ranges over an enormous area from Idaho into Mexico and Texas.

Temperature: Hot! These lizards require a basking spot of 110°F (43.3°C) and ambient daytime temperatures up to the 90s (32.2-35°C). Cooler retreats obviously are mandatory for adequate thermoregulation; these areas should be in the mid 70s (23.3-24.4°C).

The six-lined racerunner (*C. sex-lineatus*) occurs in grasslands, open woodlands, and deserts, so it can fare well in a desert, savanna, or dry woodland terrarium.

Lighting: Ten hours or more daily of full-spectrum lighting.
Description: The whiptails encompass a very large group of lizards within the family Teiidae, which includes the large tegus of South America. Whiptails range from Wisconsin and Maryland to northern Argentina, and they are so diverse and complex that an entire book could easily be written just on them.

For our purposes, however, these lizards are large and muscular with thickly plated scales atop their heads and small plated scales on the back. The lateral surfaces of many species are weakly scaled in tiny velvet-like scales, while the ventral surface is again plated in thick scales.

The snout draws to a sharp point and the eyes are large, indicating that these animals employ their sight primarily when lunging forward to snag prey. The feet are often flanged to afford the animal additional traction when running. The long, stiff tail acts as a counterbalance when the animal needs additional speed. A whiptail may run completely upright on its hind legs at speeds in excess of 15 miles (24.1 km) per hour. Specially adapted to high-speed flight, these lizards are exceptionally nervous. Obviously, this tendency toward being so high-strung makes whiptails a group of lizards that are better kept for observation and aesthetic purposes. Most whiptails can inflict painful, bloody bites on careless keepers.
Pet Suitability: 3. Whiptails are beautiful and often inexpensive lizards that unfortunately make poor captives. Specimens are very frequently imported with massive parasite loads and must be treated by a skilled veterinarian. Some species are hardier than others, but they still have demanding needs for heat, light, and space.

Savanna Species

The savanna-style terrarium is one that mimics life on the border lands between desert and forest, steppe, or grassland. From the dusty plains of Africa to the breadbasket of the American Mid-West, savannas exist virtually worldwide. Savannas are dry, yet they sport far more vegetation than their slightly more arid cousins, the deserts. Like deserts, savannas sustain considerably more species of reptile life than the common observer might suspect. Because savannas exist at the nexus between drier and wetter areas of habitat, most species hailing from these regions are hardy and resilient when it comes to relative humidity needs. This is not an excuse for the hobbyist to be lax in properly maintaining his or her terrarium environment, but it is to say that the animals found in the savanna habitat tend to be more "forgiving" of some of the husbandry miscalculations. Thus a wide range of excellent "starter" lizards hail from the world's savannas.

Ameiva (*Ameiva ameiva*)

Range: Central America. Introduced to Miami-Dade County, Florida.

Size: Speculative; reports of specimens in excess of 36 inches (91.4 cm) continue to surface, though many hobbyists claim that 24 inches (61 cm) is adult maximum.

Diet: Insects and small vertebrates, including rodents and fledgling birds.

Longevity: May exceed eight years.

Terrarium Size: As large as possible. Like their relatives the whiptails, all ameivas require very spacious enclosures. Custom-built pens or outdoor enclosures are preferable.

Ameivas are delicate in captivity. They require very large enclosures, strong lighting, and plenty of food.

Temperatures: Ambient temperatures in the low 80s (26.7-28.3°C) with multiple basking spots of 105°-110° F (40.6-43.3°C). Nightly temperatures should not drop below the mid 70s (23.3-24.4°C), as this tropical species needs its warmth.

Lighting: 12-14 hours daily of full-spectrum;

unfiltered natural sunlight is also highly recommended.

Description: One of the larger members of the family Teiidae, the ameiva has highly honed senses designed for helping the lizard hunt prey in darkness as it stalks through subterranean mammal burrows (and these heightened senses make this lizard *very* nervous and skittish in captivity). Coloration ranges from tan to brown with emerald and aquamarine highlights, which are particularly prevalent along the tail and hindquarters. The head is long and the snout is pointed for rooting out burrowing prey. The scales are heavy and closely linked, giving the lizard a plate mail-like covering. The eyes and ear openings are very large, testaments to this lizard's reliance on its keen senses. At full run, the ameiva can move surprisingly fast. Adept at climbing, the ameiva is just at home in low branches as on the ground. Basks frequently and makes deep burrows.

Pet Suitability: 5. Ameivas are imported (few, if any, are captive bred) and carry heavy internal parasite loads, so these animals have an incredibly high mortality rate once they enter the pet trade. Only the most skilled of lizard keepers should attempt to keep this beautiful, yet fragile and demanding, animal.

Armadillo Lizard (*Cordylus* spp.)

Range: Southern Africa.

Size: Large adults seldom exceed 8 inches (20.3 cm).

Diet: All manner of invertebrates. In captivity, dusted crickets and gut-loaded mealworms are excellent staples.

Longevity: May exceed 15 years.

Terrarium Size: 15-gallon (56.8-l) minimum. Because these lizards naturally thrive in colonies

Several species of armadillo lizards (*C. cataphractus* in this photo) roll into a ball when threatened.

When in breeding condition, the head of a male broadhead skink takes on a red to orange color.

of several individuals, it is advisable to maintain three to five lizards in a 30-gallon (113.6-l) or larger terrarium. Armadillo lizards will be content in a desert or savanna setup.

Temperatures: Daily ambient temperatures in the low to mid 80s (26.7-29.4°C) with a basking spot of up to 95° F (35°C) is best. They tolerate and probably appreciate a large temperature drop at night.

Lighting: 8 to 12 hours of full-spectrum light.

Description: Perhaps the smallest of the girdle-tailed lizards ever to appear on the pet market, the armadillo lizard wears a plate mail coat of thick ridged scales along its flanks, limbs, and dorsum, and it sports even more heavily armored scales down the length of its tail. The bony head is similarly armored. Coloration is ruddy brown to rust dorsally with whitish to cream on the vent. Several species are imported and a few are captive bred.

When fleeing from prey, the armadillo lizard has two defense strategies. The first is to wedge itself into a tight crevice and "puff up" by gulping huge amounts of air so that the predator cannot extract the lizard from its nook. The second defense strategy, which appears nowhere else in the lizard world, is to curl itself up into a ball and grasp its tail in its mouth, such that it forms a very inedible-looking ball of spikes and spurs. Communal by nature, armadillo lizards often live in very close proximity to one another.

Pet Suitability: 1. Hardy, durable, and strangely cute, these rugged little reptiles are also easily cared for and seldom refuse to feed in captivity. Live-bearing animals, they make an excellent choice for the novice or young hobbyist, as well as a unique breeding challenge for the more advanced lizard keeper. I wholeheartedly recommend armadillo lizards to any reptile enthusiast.

Broadhead Skink (*Eumeces laticeps*)

Range: Found throughout American Southeast and Mid-West

Size: Up to 12.5 inches (31.8 cm)

Diet: Insects. May also take occasional bits of fruit and dandelion heads.

Longevity: Ten years or more.

Terrarium Size: These skinks like their floor space; nothing smaller than 40-gallons (151.4-l) is recommended for adult specimens.

Temperatures: Ambient in low 80s (26.7-28.3°C) with basking spot of 100° F (37.8°C). Cooler retreats mandatory.

Lighting: Full-spectrum lighting for 10 to 12 hours daily.

Description: A heavy-bodied species, the adult broadhead skink has a uniform color of golden to burnished copper. Older individuals may turn grayish. The head, however, of this otherwise bland-looking reptile is flaming red to reddish orange, making it an unusually attractive species. The jaws, strapped with powerful musculature, extend beyond the edges of the neck, giving the head a roughly triangular shape. Young are black with five to seven

Male (above) and female (below) fire skinks. Treating a wild-caught fire skink for parasites is critical to successfully keeping it.

longitudinal yellow stripes down a black body and a brilliant blue tail. Males of the species are larger and have a brighter, wider head than do females, and may sport extra-vibrant coloration during the breeding season (April-July).

Broadhead skinks enjoy deep cover in their terrariums: slabs of cork bark, plenty of vegetation, dark hides, etc. Devout baskers, especially during the early morning, these lizards will definitely benefit from exposure to UV bulbs. Startled skinks, or those that have suddenly and unexpectedly been picked up, can bite hard!

Pet Suitability: 2. Although not as pet-friendly as some species, this animal is hardy and impressive, making a great display lizard. It typically has a more congenial, mellow disposition after becoming acclimated to the sights and sounds of its keeper and environment.

Fat-Tailed Gecko (*Hemitheconyx caudicinctus*)

Range: African savannas and semi-arid regions.

Size: Up to 8 inches (20.3 cm)

Diet: Insects; calcium and D3 supplements should be added to every to every other feeding.

Longevity: May exceed 15-20 years.

Terrarium Size: Fat-tailed geckos are terrestrial geckos. An adult fat-tailed gecko can be adequately housed in a 15-gallon (56.8-l) terrarium. As is true with the other terrestrial geckos, terrarium height is of negligible importance. Having a humidified hiding area is highly recommended.

Temperatures: Provide a thermal gradient of 75°F (23.9°C) at one end of the terrarium to the upper 80s (30.5-31°C) at the other. Because of their nocturnal lifestyle, fat-tailed geckos rarely bask for long periods of time.

Lighting: 10-14 hours per day; photoperiod is particularly important if you are planning a breeding project with your geckos. Ultraviolet light is not necessary (rarely necessary with any lizard species that is primarily nocturnal), but it is advisable.

Description: Close cousins to the ever-popular leopard gecko, the fat-tailed gecko is a terrestrial thick-bodied and slow-moving animal that seems to be in a perpetually pleasant mood. Fat-tailed geckos, like all other eublepharids, have moveable eyelids.

Coloration is highly variable, but virtually all specimens wear a mottled coat of brownish purple to reddish or maroon with paler

Five More Savanna Lizards

banded velvet gecko (*Homopholis fasciata*)
fence lizard (*Sceloporus undulatus*)
frilled lizard (*Chlamydosaurus kingii*)
South American swifts (*Liolaemus* species)
velvet gecko (*Oedura castelnaui*)

Pair of fat-tailed geckos; the male normally is larger than the female and has a wider head.

lavender to purplish blotches. Selective breeding projects have produced color and pattern variants, including albino, leucistic, and patternless.

Fat-tailed geckos may be housed in small colonies without problems just so long as rival males are not kept in close proximity to one another. A viable colony is best composed of a single male and several females. Males are distinguishable from females based on the presence of up to nine femoral pores just anterior to the vent or cloaca, as well as having larger heads and overall body size.

Pet Suitability: 1. The fat-tailed gecko is an excellent starter lizard; I recommend it to hobbyists of any experience level. These lizards are cute, very docile, and quite hardy and long lived. Like their leopard gecko cousins, they seem to enjoy to be taken out and held, especially when they are adults, although some are a bit more nervous than the average leopard gecko.

A Skink by Any Other Name

There is some debate about which genus the fire skink belongs in. Some authorities consider it a member of *Riopa* instead of *Lygosoma,* and it is also occasionally listed under *Mochlus.* This is something the keeper should be aware of when looking up additional information on this lizard.

Fire Skink (*Lygosoma fernandi*)

Range: Tropical Africa.

Size: To 12 inches (30.5 cm).

Diet: Grubs and gut-loaded mealworms (and superworms) are recommended captive fare. May also take occasional bits of fruit, dandelion heads, and canned dog food.

Longevity: Ten years or more.

Terrarium Size: Large; nothing smaller than 40-gallon (151.4-l) terrarium will suffice for an adult; 55-gallons (208.2-l) or larger is advisable. Make sure to include many moist hideaways in the fire skink's terrarium, as these animals need access to both moist and dry environs.

Temperatures: Ambient of low 80s (26.7-28.3°C) with basking spot of 95° F (35°C).

Lighting: Eight to ten hours of full-spectrum lighting.

Description: As its name suggests, this skink is orange to reddish golden, mottling toward the tail, and the flanks are ablaze in splotches of vibrant red interspaced with black, white, and golden scales. The upper jaw and cheeks are red and the chin is zebra-striped. Juveniles are even more dashingly patterned than adults. Fond of early morning and afternoon basking, the fire skink spends its days rooting through the underbrush in search of its favorite prey: grubs.

When constructing a fire skink terrarium, it is important to note that while these lizards come from savanna and forest environments, they never stray far from permanent sources of water. Large water dishes and moistened hideaways are a must within the fire skink terrarium; it may be best to think of them as forest lizards rather than savanna dwellers. You should provide these skinks with a substrate they can burrow in.

Pet Suitability: 3. In some hobbyists' experience, fire skinks are perhaps the world's perfect mix of beauty and hardiness, but others have experienced less success with them. Personally, I find they thrive best in naturalistic environs such as living vivariums or natural terrariums. Wild-collected specimens tend to suffer from internal parasite loads, however, and should be inspected by a skilled reptile veterinarian as soon as possible.

Great Plains Skink (*Eumeces obsoletus*)

Range: Extensive throughout the American West and Mid-West into northern Mexico.

Size: Largest skink in North America; may exceed 13 inches (33 cm) long.

Diet: Insects. Dust every other meal with calcium supplement. May also take occasional bits of fruit and dandelion heads. Like most other large skinks, this species may eat canned dog food, and adults relish the occasional pinkie mouse offered as a treat.

Longevity: May exceed 12 years.

Terrarium Size: As large as

Helmeted geckos will thrive in desert or savanna terrariums when provided with humidified burrows.

Until 2002, the helmeted gecko was the sole member of the genus *Geckonia*. A detailed DNA analysis of this creature revealed that it is so closely related to *Tarentola* that it should be considered a member of that genus. The older name is still widely used.

possible, as this mammoth skink enjoys roaming about wide open spaces. I recommend against anything less than 55-gallons (208.2-l).

Temperatures: Daily ambient of low 80s (26.7-28.3°C) with basking spot to 100° F (37.8°C). Nightly drops of up to 20° F (11°C) are acceptable.

Lighting: 10-12 hours of full-spectrum is recommended.

Description: Adults wear a yellowish to coppery-golden base coloration with darker brown to burnished bronze-colored posterior edges on each dorsal scale; these dark edges more or less align to form oblique rows across and down the dorsum. The belly and flanks are yellow to cream colored. Juveniles are jet black with bluish to white spots along the jaws and flanks.

The body is torpedo shaped and sleek; head is wedge shaped and is equipped with very powerful jaw muscles. If cornered or harassed, these skinks will not hesitate to bite *hard*. Fond of early morning and late afternoon basking. Like many other skinks, Great Plains skinks need burrowing opportunities in captivity.

Pet Suitability: 3. So far as a showpiece skink goes, the Great Plains skink is hard to beat, but there are any number of more handle-friendly species on the market. If housed under proper conditions, the Great Plains skink is a hardy captive indeed. It rarely refuses food and adjusts to captivity with few other problems.

Helmeted Gecko (*Tarentola chazaliae*)

Range: Coastal North Africa.

Size: 3.5 inches (8.9 cm).

Diet: Small insects. Captives relish two-week-old crickets and small mealworms as well as mealworm beetles.

Longevity: Five years or more is not uncommon.

Terrarium Size: 10-gallon (37.9-l) minimum for a pair, though 15-gallons (56.8-l) is recommended.

Temperatures: Daily from 85°-94° (29.4-34.4°C) with cooler retreats. Nighttime temps should dip into the mid 70s (23.3-24.4°C).

Lighting: 12-14 hours of full-spectrum is recommended, although these lizards seldom bask.

Description: Unique among gecko species, the helmeted gecko is a very small species indeed. With small knobby scales and yellowish coloration flecked with patches of white and gray, the nocturnal/crepuscular helmeted gecko can literally disappear in plain sight when sitting motionless amidst a sandy, rocky backdrop. The enlarged conical scales at the base of the skull grant this lizard its common name.

This lizard requires a desert or savanna terrarium with humidified hiding areas. Occasional misting is recommended, and the keeper should make sure that his or her helmeted geckos do not retain shed skin, a common problem for this species.

Pet Suitability: 2. The helmeted gecko is a hardy, durable species that can thrive in a colony of its own kind. A hobbyist who is skilled in desert or savanna species should have no problem maintaining one or more of these animals, though a beginning hobbyist should look elsewhere for a first lizard.

Long-Tailed Grass Lizard (*Takydromus sexlineatus*)

Range: Southern China, Southeast Asia, Sumatra.

Size: Adults may grow to 14 inches (35.6 cm) long—the tail being five times the body length—but they stay very slender-bodied throughout their life.

Diet: Small crickets and grasshoppers primarily. Captive specimens may also take small mealworms and roaches. Dust every other meal.

Longevity: Four years or more is not uncommon.

Terrarium Size: Long-tailed grass lizards are active animals with a need for spacious environs. Fortunately, because they are so small, their terrarium can be relatively small, yet still "spacious" enough for these demure lizards. One or two

The long-tailed grass lizard's tail helps it balance when moving across long stems of grass.

Like other swifts, pink-bellies often perch on tall rocks or fence posts to keep watch for both prey and predators.

lizards will thrive in a 20-gallon (75.7-l) enclosure. More lizards will require a larger tank. They do best in a tall cage with lots of climbing branches.

Temperatures: Ambient in the high 70s to low 80s (25.6-28.3°C) with a basking spot to mid 90s F (34.4-35.6°C).

Lighting: 10-12 hours per day; full-spectrum lighting is recommended but probably not mandatory.

Description: A diurnal hunter, the long-tailed grass lizard is indeed a very elongate animal; its tail is typically five times the length of the rest of its body. This long tail aids the reptile by evenly distributing it weight as it stalks through the tops of weeds, tall grasses, and bamboo. Despite the earth tones of brown, tan, and yellowish to white that adorn the dorsum, flanks, and vent of this species, the long-tailed grass lizard is a surprisingly handsome species.

This animal has keen eyesight, hearing, and a very long spearpoint-like snout, which it uses for lancing prey between blades of grass or weedy stalks. Active primarily in the early morning and late afternoons, this lizard avoids the extreme heat of day by seeking out a rock crevice or lying quietly in deep vegetation. Long-tailed grass lizards are equally at home in a savanna or forest terrarium.

Pet Suitability: 1. One of my personal favorites among savanna-dwelling species, the long-tailed grass lizard is the perfect mix of interesting, attractive, and charming. Because of their fragile limbs and tails, these lizards are for watching only, but their seemingly friendly disposition makes them a heartwarming reptile nonetheless.

Moorish Gecko (*Tarentola mauritanica*)

Range: Israel, southern Europe, and western Middle East.

Size: A large adult may attain 6 inches (15.2 cm).

Diet: Insects. Captive fare should be as varied as possible.

Longevity: Seven years or more is not uncommon.

Terrarium Size: One adult can thrive in a 15-gallon (56.8-l) tank, though the staunchly arboreal nature of the species makes the height of the terrarium far more important than total floor space. Will do well in a desert or savanna setup.

Temperatures: Upper 70s to mid 80s (25.6-29.4°C). Basking light is not necessary.

Lighting: Full-spectrum lighting is not absolutely necessary but may be beneficial.

Description: The Moorish gecko—also called the crocodile gecko—has a flat head with pronounced jaws, giving the head a triangular appearance. The grayish to near-white body is covered in tubercles and granular scales arranged in longitudinal rows; scales are elongate and spine-like along the tail. As in most other gecko species, the toe pads are broad and adhesive, allowing the Moorish gecko to cling to virtually all surfaces. Only the third and fourth toes sport tiny claws. The pupils of the eyes are slit and the iris is reticulated, two adaptations indicative of this animal's nocturnal habits.

The Moorish gecko makes a very hardy pet when kept in a desert or savanna terrarium.

Hunting insects by night (especially around street lights and billboards), this lizard spends its days tucked safely within loose tree bark or amid rocky crevices. May squeak or hold mouth agape when agitated; has a bad bite for its size. Multiple males kept in the same enclosure will fight to the death; males are distinguished from females by the presence of enlarged femoral pores just anterior the vent.

Pet Suitability: 1. Although not the most handle-friendly pet lizard on the market, the Moorish gecko is a stalwart, rugged, and quietly attractive specimen that can make an excellent addition to any captive lizard collection.

Pink-Bellied Swift (*Sceloporus variabilis*)

Range: Extreme southern Texas south through Costa Rica.

Size: Large adults seldom attain 6 inches (15.2 cm).

Diet: Favors grasshoppers and locusts in the wild, so gut-loaded crickets are an excellent alternative in captivity. Offer a variety of insects.

Longevity: May exceed eight years.

Terrarium Size: Pink-bellied swifts enjoy vertical as well as horizontal space; a 30- to 36-gallon (113.6-136.3-l) tank would be a good choice.

Temperatures: Ambient of mid 80s (28.9-30°C) with basking spot of no more than 100°F (37.8°C). Nightly dips into the low 70s (21.1-22.7°C) are acceptable.

Lighting: 10-12 hours of full-spectrum lighting recommended.

Description: Another of the hardier members of the genus *Sceloporus*, the pink-bellied swift (also called the rose-bellied swift) is a small, rough-scaled lizard that derives its common name from the pinkish to rosy-colored patches that occur along its flanks and belly. These patches are bordered with a dark blue. A pronounced blue spot is also commonly present just behind the forelimbs. Dorsum is light brown to greenish with a faint dorsolateral stripe.

A Lizard of a Different Color

One of the first things that many readers notice right away about this book is that it lacks information on the true chameleons. This is not an oversight. Simply stated, true chameleons are a diverse and intriguing group of reptiles about which there is a lot to be said. They have very specialized feeding, watering, and ventilation requirements in captivity. The long and the short of it is that chameleons are more than deserving of a book devoted entirely to them, and they are best left to the most experienced hobbyists.

Highly arboreal, the pink-bellied swift spends the lion's share of its time perched atop fence posts or on the sides of trees or mesquite bushes.

Pet Suitability: 1. One of the hardiest of all *Sceloporus* species, the pink-bellied swift adapts well to captivity.

Schneider's Skink (*Eumeces schneideri schneideri*)

Range: Northern Africa; other subspecies range into the Middle East and Central Asia.

Size: To 12 inches (30.5 cm)

Diet: Insects; adults may also take the occasional pinkie mouse. May accept canned lizard chow, vegetables, and fruit.

Longevity: Speculated to be over 15 years.

Terrarium Size: 55-gallons (208.2-l) for one or more adults. Needs a dry terrarium with humidified shelters.

Temperatures: Daily ambient of 83-86° F (28.3-30°C) with hot spots to 100° (37.8°C). Cooler burrows are necessary, and nighttime temperatures can drop to the low 60s (15.6-17.2°C).

Schneider's skink is one of several skinks that will eat canned cat and dog foods in captivity.

Lighting: 10-12 hours of full-spectrum lighting.

Description: A husky, powerful, and semi-aggressive lizard, Schneider's skink has a base color of slate to silvery gray. The ventral surface is yellowish to cream. Bright orange flecks pepper the dorsum in broken lateral rows. The midline of the flank is adorned in this orange hue, and the legs are speckled in orange as well. The very handsomest specimens have nearly red speckling and a deep gray base color. The Berber skink (*Eumeces schneideri algeriensis*) is one of the most colorful and available subspecies.

Diurnal hunters, these lizards both run down their prey as well as root it out of crevices and from under loose leaf litter. If cornered or threatened, Schneider's skink will bite!

Pet Suitability: 1. Despite some hobbyists' claims that Schneider's skink is semi-aggressive, I have not found this to be the case. These skinks are curious, inquisitive animals that frequently approach the glass of their terrariums to be fed or taken out and handled.

Rugged and hardy, these tough lizards are amazingly beautiful, long-lived, and durable in captivity. Virtually all specimens are wild-caught, however and must be inspected at once for possible internal parasite infestation.

Forest Species

When I hear the word "woodland," my knee-jerk reaction is to visualize the ferny creek banks and laurel-clad hillsides of my own native homeland, the Appalachian Mountains of northern Georgia. However, "woodlands" encompass far more biomes than just the hills and dales around my own home. Africa has many non-tropical hardwood forests, as does Asia and much of Europe, and virtually all of these forested areas support different species of lizards that can all thrive under similar conditions.

The common attributes of the forested areas of the world that lizard keepers should understand are thicker, richer soil; heavier ground cover; and more lush plant life than either the desert or the savanna ecosystem. The soil is normally covered by leaf litter. Keep the relative humidity above 50 percent in a woodland tank and you should have few problems managing the lizard species that thrive therein.

Mysterious *Mabuya*

Currently, the genus *Mabuya* is perhaps the most twisted, muddled, and confusing mess of nomenclature and speciation within the entire pet reptile field. Collectors give incorrect names to importers; importers guess at what they ship out to distributors; distributors have no idea what geographic region the skinks came from, so they sell to pet shops under best-guess names; and pet shops slap a catchy name on the terrarium animal to sell to the hobbyist. By the time the hobbyist enters into the equation, there is basically no way of knowing what species is being sold. The added complication is that many *Mabuya* closely resemble each other.

Luckily, the husbandry requirements of one of these species is, by and large, adequate for most species that may appear in the pet trade, and many are hardy animals. If you purchase one of these mystery skinks, observe it keenly to see whether you are providing the right conditions. Overall, these are excellent pet lizards for beginners and more experienced hobbyists alike.

African Woodland Skinks (*Mabuya* spp.)

Range: Extensive and fragmented throughout Africa, Asia, and tropical Americas. Widely introduced into new areas via shipping and pet industry escapees and releases. Most of those available in the hobby originate in tropical Africa.

Size: Variable depending on the species in question; some may reach 12 inches (30.5 cm) though most are somewhat smaller.

Diet: Insects; some species may take sweet fruits and other vegetation.

Longevity: Five years on average.

Terrarium Size: Terrarium size will vary based on the size of the species you have. These skinks are not wide-roaming or overly active animals, so they will not require

A number of different *Mabuya* species are imported from Africa, all confusingly similar. These are identified as the orange-flanked skink (*M. perrotetii*) and the elegant skink (*M. elegans*). Note the forked tail of the elegant skink, indicating the tail was once lost and regenerated

an expansive unit. A 15-gallon (56.8-l) enclosure may suffice for a single individual or a pair of small specimens, while a larger terrarium will be necessary for a small colony.

Temperatures: Variable depending on the exact geographic origin of the species in question. Suggested temperatures are ambient in low 80s (26.7-28.3°C) with basking spot to 100° F (37.8°C) with a nightly drop to low 70s (21-22.8°C).

Lighting: 8-12 hours of full-spectrum lighting.

Description: Highly variable, though all species have a roughly torpedo-shaped body with reduced limbs, pointed nose, and tightly overlying small scales. Eyes are also reduced in most species, as their subterranean lifestyle calls only minimally on eyesight. Coloration ranges from solid black with white dorsal stripes and speckles laterally in *M. striata* to tan with red flanks and turquoise speckles in *M. perroteti*. All species are baskers; they emerge from dark recesses of stone or wood early in the morning to bask before moving off to hunt prey. All drink both standing water from puddles and lap droplets; many receive ample water from their prey items, though a water supply should always be kept at your animals' disposal.

Most species of *Mabuya* can be housed communally with others of their own species. Some of the most popularly imported species include the striped African skink *(M. striata)*, the African blue-tailed skink *(M. quinequecarinata)*, the Kalahari skink *(M. spilogaster),* and the rainbow or orange-flanked skink *(M. perroteti)*. If you are keeping a skink of unknown origin, watch its behavior carefully and adjust your husbandry if it seems to be doing poorly.

Pet Suitability: 2. Overall, these are hardy and attractive reptiles that can make excellent beginner species.

Bibron's Gecko *(Pachydactylus bibroni)*

Range: Southern Africa.

Size: To 6 inches (15.2 cm); exceptionally large animals may reach 9 inches (22.9 cm).

Diet: Insects.

Longevity: Usually over five years.

Terrarium Size: Like most other nocturnal geckos, Bibron's requires little in terms of terrarium size; 10 gallons (37.9 l) will suffice. One or two hidden vertical retreats are all it needs, as this arboreal animal will utilize the entire vertical surface area of the terrarium's glass.

Temperatures: Ambient in the low to mid 80s (26.7-30°C). Can tolerate lower nighttime temperatures.

Lighting: No special lighting necessary.

Description: A small, quietly attractive lizard, Bibron's gecko sports a coat of tiny granular scales and fleshy protuberances. Coloration is gray to tan

Male anoles sport an extendable dewlap under the chin that is used in territorial and mating displays. The dewlap of the brown anole is generally an orange-red color.

with some dorsal striping and ringing around the tail; particularly handsome specimens may have pinkish hues among the legs and dorsum. As in most other geckos, eggs may be visible through the belly skin of gravid females.

Pet Suitability: 1. Although not very handle-friendly (few arboreal geckos are), Bibron's is a hale and hardy animal that can make an excellent introduction to the keeping of arboreal geckos.

A female green anole basks on fern leaf in Hawaii. Green anoles were accidentally introduced to Hawaii and now thrive there.

Brown Anole (*Anolis sagrei*)

Range: Native to Caribbean Islands. Introduced to southern and eastern Florida.

Size: May reach 8.5 inches (21.6 cm) or slightly larger.

Diet: Insects. Vary captive diet and supplement every other meal. Water both by supplying with a dish and by dripping or misting water onto the walls of the terrarium daily, as this lizard enjoys lapping up tiny droplets off leaves and other environs.

Longevity: Five to eight years

Terrarium Size: As is true of all 300 known species of anole known, the brown anole prefers vertical climbing space over lateral or horizontal space. A tall tank is mandatory. A single specimen may thrive in a 10-gallon (37.9 l) tank; a colony of three or more will require roughly 10 gallons (37.9 l) of room each, so a three-lizard colony would need a 30-gallon (113.6-l) tank.

Temperatures: Daily ambient of low 80s (26.7-28.3°C) with a hot spot of 95°F (35°C). Cooler shady retreats are a must.

Lighting: 10-12 hours of full-spectrum florescent.

Description: The brown anole wears a dorsal coat of brown to gray with lighter speckles of whitish to cream along dorsum and flanks. Midline of the back may also sport a paler jagged streak. There are a number of subspecies, so the pattern and color vary. The male's throat fan (or dewlap)—a common feature of anoles—is yellow to orange with bead-like protuberances of black. Head is wedge-shaped.

Like other anoles, the brown anole is diurnal. Hardy and quietly attractive, this lizard does well in small groups and seldom refuses food. Unless using a very large terrarium, house only one male per cage. This adaptable lizard will often do well in a rainforest or savanna setting as well.

Other beautiful and desirable anoles that may be cared for like the brown anole include the bark anole *(A. distichus)*, the large-headed anole *(A. cybotes)*, and the crested anole (*Anolis cristatellus*). **Pet Suitability:** 2. Like other common anoles, the brown anole is hardy, but it is often poorly cared for because it is small and inexpensive. Also, because of its small size, it may be a challenge to find appropriately sized feeder insects in some areas. Generally, two-week-old crickets and similar-sized insects are acceptable. Although not the most "handle-friendly" of lizard species (small and jumpy), the brown anole does make an excellent pet for a new hobbyist.

Female house gecko with eggs visibly developing in her abdomen.

Green Anole (*Anolis carolinensis*)

Range: Extensive throughout the American South. Introduced to Japan and other Pacific islands.

Size: 5 to 8 inches (12.7-20.3 cm).

Diet: Small insects. Water both by supplying with a dish and by dripping or misting water onto the walls of the terrarium daily, as this lizard enjoys lapping up tiny droplets off leaves and other surfaces. Supplement every other meal.

Longevity: May exceed five years.

Terrarium Size: Devoutly arboreal, green anoles prefer vertical space to horizontal, so a tall tank is more important than a wide one. A 30-gallon (113.6-l) enclosure is suitable for hosting a small colony of green anoles, while one or two will be fine in 10 gallons (37.8 l)

Temperatures: Ambient in the mid 70s (23.3-25°C) with basking spot to mid 90s, (34.4-35.6°C).

Lighting: Eight to ten hours of full-spectrum fluorescent.

Description: One of the small iguanid lizards of North America, the green anole is a highly arboreal lizard with a pointed head, long tail, moderately adhesive toe pads (coupled with small claws), and the ability to change color within a limited range—pale to emerald green, brown, and gray.

Both males and females have a reddish to pink dewlap, but dewlaps are greatly enlarged in males. When courting a female or contesting against rival males, a male green anole will head-bob or do "push-ups" on the side of a tree or other arboreal perch and flare his dewlap, sometimes holding it erect for several seconds at a time.

Diurnal hunters, green anoles have keen eyesight and often leap considerable distances from branch to branch or from branch to the ground in order to pounce on their prey. They are capable of catching flying insects on the wing.

Pet Suitability: 2. See comments for the brown anole, as they apply here as well. A small colony of green anoles (or a mixed colony containing multiple species of anoles) thriving in a living

So Many Anoles

The green anole has always been and continues to be a staple of the pet trade. Green anoles are now found in the company of several relatives; wide varieties of anoles are now available to the public. There are over 100 species of anole in the Caribbean Islands alone. Many of these species are frequently encountered in neighborhood shops, while others, such as *Anolis smallwoodi*, may be available only through specialty dealers. There are even a number of hobbyists (mostly in Europe) breeding odd species of anoles. If you live in the right geographic area, or you will be taking a trip to south Florida, you may even have an opportunity to collect your anoles from the wild. Make sure to check all state and local laws before doing so, however, to ensure that you are not breaking any laws in collecting your lizards. Whatever your fancy, and however you go about obtaining it, there is certainly an anole out there for everyone!

As Plain as Day

There is so very much that needs to be said about day geckos that no small section devoted to them in a book like this could sufficiently cover what the average hobbyist needs to know in order to successfully keep and maintain them. With over 25 species currently appearing with some degree of regularity in the pet trade, it is easy to see how these little lizards warrant an entire book dedicated to them. If these lizards interest you, I suggest you research as much as you can on the topic.

vivarium can make a spectacular showpiece terrarium.

House Gecko (*Hemidactylus* spp.)

Range: Native to southern Asia and the Pacific Rim, introduced widely throughout Florida, the Caribbean, and other areas.

Size: To 5 inches (12.7 cm).

Diet: Small insects. Water by misting the terrarium walls at dusk.

Longevity: Four years or a bit longer.

Terrarium Size: This lizard may spend its entire life hunting up and down the bark of a single tree or among the nooks and crannies of a single length of stone wall. Offer plenty of vertical structure; a 10-gallon (37.9-l) tank turned on end works well to support up to three individuals. House geckos will also do well in a rainforest terrarium.

Temperatures: Ambient in mid 80s (28.9-30°C).

Lighting: No special lighting necessary.

Description: Small, fleet footed, and acutely aware of its surroundings, the house gecko is seldom caught napping by predators. Unfortunately for it, its primary line of defense is to rely on its camouflage for protection, sitting perfectly motionless and hoping to go unnoticed. Spending its days tucked away in a building's cracked wall or under a slab of loose bark, this gecko emerges at dusk to hunt insects. Utters an audible squeak or "bark" when disturbed or fighting. No mating is involved within several species of this genus; as a curious adaptation rarely seen in such advanced life forms, some species asexually develop and deposit one to two eggs every year.

Pet Suitability: 2. Commonly sold as feeders for milk snakes and other lizard-eating reptiles, house geckos are typically very inexpensive, so a small colony of these nocturnal hunters is within virtually any hobbyist's fiscal reach. Because of their small size and inexpensiveness, house geckos often suffer from the same neglect that anoles do.

Rainforest Species

Take the moisture and shady overhang of the forest biome to the next level and what you come away with is the jungle or rainforest habitat. The tropical rain forests of the world play host to a seemingly endless parade of reptile and amphibian life. Many insectivorous lizards from the rainforest make it to the pet trade; lots of those that do are very specialized lizards that are tough to keep. A sampling of those that enter the pet trade and are not too difficult to keep follows.

Chinese Water Dragon (*Physignathus cocincinus*)

Range: Southeast Asia.

Size: To 36 inches (91.4 cm) though much of this is tail.

Diet: Insect, small mammals, fruit, and flowers. Requires regular vitamin/calcium supplementation in captivity.

Longevity: Ten years or more is common.

Terrarium Size: Large, this animal should have enough space to both fully stretch out and climb. A 75-gallon (283.9-l) terrarium is the minimum size for an adult; a custom-made enclosure is your best bet.

Temperatures: Ambient in upper 70s (25-26.1°C) with basking spots in mid 90s (34.4-35.6°C).

Lighting: 10-12 hours full-spectrum lighting.

Description: A large agamid lizard, the Chinese water dragon has an appearance that suits its common name. It is *very* dragon-like in that it wears an emerald green coat of fine scales and has cranial, dorsal,

The gold-dust day gecko (*P. laticauda*) is one of the most common and hardiest of the smaller day geckos.

Five More Forest Lizards

alligator lizards (*Elgaria* species)
European green lizard (*Lacerta viridis*)
panther gecko (*Paroedura pictus*)
five-lined skink (*Eumeces fasciatus*)
jeweled lizard (*Lacerta lepida*)

and tail crests that, in particularly handsome specimens, extend high off the body and are topped in a row of thin, spiny scales. Large conical scales of white to turquoise blue adorn the jaw. The common name is also appropriate in that the lizard hails from Asia and lives near or in water at virtually all times.

Chinese water dragons must be housed in a large terrarium (in cramped enclosures, these reptiles have a habit of rubbing their noses raw or even off against the screen and glass of their terrariums) and a broad water dish for soaking and drinking. They also like climbing, so the height of the terrarium is also important.

Pet Suitability: 3. One of the most frequently encountered of pet shop denizens, the Chinese water dragon is often bought on a whim, the hobbyist not fully realizing the size or water requirements of the lizard.

The coloration and irregular folds of skin grant the flying geckos excellent camouflage when resting on tree bark.

Day Geckos (*Phelsuma* spp.)

Range: Madagascar, mainland Africa. Introduced to Hawaii and other semi-tropical areas.

Size: Varies by species from 2 inches to over 14 inches (5-35.6 cm).

Diet: Insects, fruit, nectar, pollen. Apricot baby food mixed with honey and vitamin/calcium meals makes an excellent captive substitute for true nectar. Have high calcium requirements.

Longevity: Ten years or more depending on species; larger species live considerably longer than smaller ones, typically.

Terrarium Size: Variable based on the size of the species in

Dead Lizard Walking

The rainforest lizards have some members among their ranks that probably should never be kept. Either the animals are too fragile to take to captivity, are

growing increasingly scarce in the wild, or they suffer excessively during the importation process. Some such animals include lizards of the following genera: *Polychrus* (the bush anoles; *P. marmoratus* is shown at left), *Laemanctus* (coneheaded lizards), and *Corytophanes* (helmeted basilisks or forest chameleons). All of these animals are unduly fragile and rarely survive in the home terrarium, regardless of the skill level of the hobbyist.

question. All terrariums should be vertically oriented with plenty of vertical hides (cork bark slabs, for example, glued against the inside wall of the tank work very well).

Temperatures: Ambient in high 70s to low 80s (25-28°C). Basking spot to 90° F (32.2°C). Nightly drops to upper 60s (19.4-20.6°C) are acceptable.

Lighting: 12-14 hours of full-spectrum light daily.

Description: Living collages of color, these vibrant, peaceful reptiles spend their days basking in the tropical sun, munching on insects and lapping up the nectar and pollen of tropical plants. Exact coloration depends on the species and age of the specimen in question; juveniles often look nothing like their parents. Most of the species in the hobby are neon green with bright red, orange, or turquoise markings.

Staunchly arboreal and highly territorial, these lizards often stake out their favorite trees by basking on them in the classic head-down position; they may bask, stalk prey, and search for mates all while keeping an eye out for territorial rivals.

Pet Suitability: 2-4, varying according to species. Madagascar giants *(P. madagascariensis grandis),* for example, are stunning, long-lived animals that I would rank at 2, while the appropriately named neon day gecko *(P. klemmeri)* can be more challenging, and might rank at 4. The common small species, such as the gold dust day gecko *(P. laticauda)* and

Five More Rainforest Lizards

brown water dragon (*Physignathus lesuerii*)
crested gecko (*Rhacodactylus ciliatus*)
garden lizards (*Calotes* species)
green-eyed gecko (*Gekko smithii*)
Timor monitor (*Varanus timorensis*)

the lined day gecko *(P. lineata)*, fall in the middle, being a 3 mainly because their small size requires that the keeper feed them tiny insects. Over 25 species now appear for sale in the U.S. pet trade, so do your homework on the exact species you desire before making a purchase.

Flying Gecko *(Ptyochozoon* spp.)

Range: Southeast Asia.
Size: To 7 inches (17.8 cm).
Diet: Insects
Longevity: May exceed ten years.
Terrarium Size: Small to moderate with emphasis on vertical height and climbing branches; a 10-gallon (37.9-l) tank or larger will suffice.
Temperatures: Upper 70s to low 80s (25-28°C) ambient. Basking spot not necessary.
Lighting: No special lighting necessary.
Description: If this lizard truly took its name from its ability to sail through the air from one tree to the next, it should be called a *gliding* gecko, as it is not capable of true flight. When cornered or in pursuit of prey, a flying gecko will leap headlong into the air, extending flaps of skin beneath its limbs and flanks, and glide to a lower perch in a nearby tree. If you want to ever see this behavior, a large terrarium is needed. Wearing the highly camouflaged base of marbled white, gray, black, and cream that it does, the flying gecko goes undetected by most diurnal predators anyway. The flaps of skin that allow it to glide also distort the animal's outline when at rest, granting it further camouflage. May bark or squeak to express alarm or breeding excitement.

There are several species of flying geckos, and they are confusingly similar in appearance. The two that are seen in the hobby most often are *P. lionotum* and *P. kuhli*. Caring for all species is the same, so it doesn't matter too much which species you actually have.
Pet Suitability: 1. Simply feed flying geckos appropriately supplemented foods, mist their terrariums lightly once or twice daily (or as needed), and keep them warm and they'll go on and on for years, just stalking around their terrariums, leaping, gliding, and hunting prey in some pretty amusing ways. A good lizard for the hobbyist interested in gaining some

experience with arboreal nocturnal geckos.

Green Tree Skink (*Lamprolepis smaragdina*)

Range: Southeastern Asia; Pacific Rim.

Size: Large individuals may exceed 13 inches (33 cm), though much of this is tail.

Diet: Insects; arboreal beetles and grubs are particularly enjoyed.

Longevity: Exact longevity is unknown. I've personally housed one specimen for eight years and three months, and it was already an adult of

As long as you obtain healthy ones, green tree skinks are hardy and long-lived lizards.

undetermined age when it came into my possession.

Terrarium Size: Though they are small lizards, green tree skinks need plenty of room to roam; as their name suggests, you should provide them with a vertically oriented tank with plenty of stout climbing branches and overhangs. In my personal experience, a 29-gallon (109.8-l) tall tank or larger works very well for these lizards.

Temperatures: Being native to the tropical Pacific region, this skink likes ambient temps of 80-83° F (26.7-28.3°C) with hot spots to 100°F (37.8°C) and nightly dips into the low 70s (21.1-22.8°C).

Lighting: Eight to ten hours of full-spectrum light daily.

Description: An amazingly colored animal, the green tree skink has a slick, shiny coat of green scales that look like polished flakes of emerald, a trait that earns this species its alternative moniker of emerald skink. The body is slender and is laterally compressed; couple these traits with the animal's extraordinarily long fingers, tiny but sharp claws, and semi-prehensile tail and it's easy to see why this lizard is so at home in the treetops. The eyes are large and dark, and vision is particularly acute. The head tapers into a spear-point snout,

Giants From Jamaica

Occasionally, Jamaican giant anoles (*Anolis garmani*) are imported for the pet trade. These beautiful emerald lizards can be kept much like knight anoles. However, Jamaican giants are much more nervous and prone to stress. Give them a very tall terrarium with an abundance of cover. Like the knight anoles, they often carry parasites and need treatment quickly if they are going to successfully adapt to captivity. You can occasionally find captive-bred individuals.

which the lizard uses to poke under loose shingles of bark in search of grubs, ants, and other hiding insect life. Males are typically much greener than females (which tend to be brownish or olive) and may become territorial if housed together. These lizards will drink from standing pools or droplets misted onto leaves. Maintain moderate levels of relative humidity.

Pet Suitability: 2. So gorgeous and unique is this skink that it can easily make a show-piece caliber pet, but it is one of the most handle-unfriendly species I know of. If handled even lightly, it wriggles, twists, turns, bites, and even defecates on its handler. Individuals will, however, take prey from their keeper's fingers and approach the glass when their keeper comes into the room; they simply don't like being touched.

Knight Anole (*Anolis equestris*)

Range: Native to Cuba, but thriving in south Florida since the late 1960s.

Size: To 18 inches (45.7 cm).

Diet: Insects, small vertebrates. Large adults have been reported to raid birds' nests of newly hatched young. Water by misting the terrarium daily, but also provide a water bowl.

Longevity: May exceed seven years.

Terrarium Size: 55-gallon (208.2-l) tank or larger, oriented vertically. This lizard is staunchly arboreal and needs all the vertical space it can get.

Temperatures: Ambient in upper 70s to low 80s (25-28°C). Basking spot to mid 90s (34.4-35.6°C) recommended.

Lighting: 10-12 hours full-spectrum light daily.

Description: One of the largest of all known anoles, the knight anole is indeed an impressive hulk of a reptile. With a head that is proportionally the largest of all anole species (and that head is strapped with powerful jaw muscles), the knight anole is the dominant arboreal lizard predator throughout much of its range.

Knight anoles wear a base coloration (note that this lizard has moderate color-changing abilities) of emerald to olive green to brown or grayish-yellow with yellow to cream flash marks on its flanks just behind the forelimbs. The knight anole can easily avoid detection when hiding in the tropical canopy. If cornered, this animal will present itself broadside to its attacker to inflate its apparent size. The bluff stops there, however, for if pressed further, an angry knight anole will bite savagely and hang on!

Pet Suitability: 2. If given amply sized and outfitted terrariums (lots of climbing and hiding areas) and ample heat, there should be no problems with housing a knight anole. I do not recommend this species for beginners in the hobby, as it can be temperamental. Most specimens are wild-caught and must be treated for internal parasite loads as soon as possible.

Plumed Basilisk (*Basiliscus plumifrons*)

Range: Guatemala to Costa Rica.

Size: To 30 inches (76.2 cm).

Diet: Insects, small reptiles, and rodents. Some individuals may take fish.

Longevity: 12 years or more.

Terrarium Size: As large as possible. Basilisks are rather large and very active; they require lots of vertical limbs and climbing branches and a large pool of water inside their terrarium if they are to thrive. Abundant cover is also mandatory to ease the nervousness of these high-strung reptiles.

The Other Basilisk

The plumed basilisk is not the only one of its kind to appear in the pet trade. The brown basilisk (*Basiliscus basiliscus*)—also native to Central America and introduced to southern Florida—is a smaller, somewhat less nervous captive. Growing to nearly 14 inches (35.6 cm) in captivity, brown basilisks may exceed seven years in age if offered excellent care. They can be kept like plumed basilisks.

The brown basilisk wears a chocolate brown base coat with cream to tan dorsolateral striping. All lighter markings are particularly pronounced in juvenile specimens. If you simply have to have a pet basilisk, this is the species I recommend; they are smaller than their plumed cousins, milder in temperament (generally), and seem to have something of a hardier constitution in the home terrarium.

Temperatures: Low 80s (26.7-28.3°C) ambient with basking spot to 100° F (37.8°C).

Lighting: 12-14 hours daily of full-spectrum light.

Description: Perhaps the most visually striking lizard ever to walk the earth, this glorious creature is emerald green and speckled along the flanks with droplets of aquamarine and black. Males of the species sport prominent dorsal and cranial crests of like coloration; particularly handsome specimens are so green that they are almost blue.

Known as the "Jesus lizard," the plumed basilisk has the ability to actually run across the top of a body of water to escape predators. Of course, few captive environments are large enough for this remarkable feat to occur in captivity. As might be expected, these lizards are extremely wary, and many a hobbyist has purchased one on account of its stunning beauty only to discover that he or she could not supply its needs in captivity. The plumed basilisk should be kept in a tank with three sides covered with opaque paint, plastic, or paper—this adds to the lizard's sense of security and helps prevent snout rubbing.

Plumed basilisks require spacious enclosures and lots of cover. A large outdoor cage may be best for them.

Adults tend to fade in coloration over time, though renowned reptile expert Dick Bartlett suggests that additional beta-carotene supplemented to meals may reverse this condition. Though sporting less vibrant coloration, females of the species tend toward much calmer dispositions.

Pet Suitability: 5. Unless you are an old hand at keeping large insectivorous lizards in fully living terrariums, I advise you to steer clear of the plumed basilisk. This animal is not for beginners. They are wiry, semi-aggressive, and prone to injure themselves or starve to death under less than ideal conditions.

Skunk Gecko (*Gekko vittatus*)

Range: Indo-Australian Archipelago, other Pacific islands.

Size: Seldom attains 10 inches (25.4 cm).

Diet: Insects; particularly moths and winged beetles. Drinks droplets of water misted onto leaves and terrarium walls and décor.

Longevity: Eight years or more not uncommon.

Terrarium Size: 20 gallons (75.7 l) with plenty of climbs and vertical hides is best. A vertically oriented terrarium is necessary.

Temperatures: Ambient temperature should be around 80°F (26.7°C) with a small hot spot that reaches 90-95°F (32.2-35°C).

Lighting: No special lighting necessary.

Description: Taking its common name from the single solid or broken longitudinal stripe that runs along both sides of the face, joins at the base of the neck, and runs down the midline of the back and tail, the skunk gecko—or lined gecko as it is often called—wears a base coat of brown, tan, or, in particularly handsome specimens, olive green. The tail is often mottled in broken patches of the same whitish color as the skunk-stripe, or it may be ringed in solid bands of white. The eyes are large with vertically elliptical pupils, and the toe-pads will adhere to any surface. Like most other arboreal geckos, skunk geckos should not be

Other species of basilisks beside the plumed are seen in the hobby, most frequently the brown basilisk (*B. basiliscus*).

handled and will bite if this admomition is ignored.

Pet Suitability: 1. So far as the nocturnal arboreal geckos go, this species is my personal favorite. Large enough to be easily observed and uniquely colored and patterned, this gecko is at once unique and hardy.

Tokay Gecko (*Gekko gecko*)

Range: Southeast Asia; introduced and established in many other places.

Size: To 13 inches (33 cm)

Diet: Insects, small rodents, other lizards.

Longevity: 18 years or more.

Terrarium Size: Moderate with emphasis on vertical height and climbing branches.

Temperatures: Upper 70s to low 80s (25-28°C) ambient. Basking spot not necessary.

Lighting: Nocturnal; no special lighting necessary.

Description: Wearing a purple to bluish base with crimson to maroon or even rust- colored speckles and small protuberances along its dorsum, the tokay is a very

The hardy skunk gecko makes a great display animal, but like the tokay they will bite aggressively when handled.

handsome animal indeed. The eyes are large, with vertically elliptical pupils (a testament to the animal's nocturnal habits), and the inside of the mouth is a deep purple as well. The ventral surface is pale bluish to white, sometimes with faint maroon spots. The tail is often banded. Toe pads cling to virtually all surfaces, even glass. The tokay is one of the most vocal geckos and may bark loudly if disturbed or prior to mating. Captive breeding efforts are raising tokays both for the pet trade and as a food and medicine source for use in many Asian cultures. Several captive-bred color varieties are starting to become available.

Pet Suitability: 2. I would like to rate the tokay gecko as a #1, because it is hardy and beautiful, but I cannot; this is one mean lizard! If allowed to live strictly as a display animal, it is an excellent choice, but the foolhardy hobbyist who makes the mistake of placing his or her hands on a tokay will soon learn just how hard this lizard can bite.